MW01065624

Black Belts Only:
The Invisible but Lethal Power of Karate

Adam Newhouse

IMPORTANT DISCLAIMERS

The techniques, concepts and ideas demonstrated and discussed in this book and any accompanying videos and materials are extremely dangerous and attempts to use or apply them in practice may result in severe injuries, bodily harm or death. If you choose to practice, follow, imitate or experiment with these techniques, concepts or ideas, you do so entirely at your own risk, and the author, publisher and all others involved in this book's creation disclaim any and all liability for any resulting damage, bodily injuries or deaths.

The opinions expressed in this book are, unless otherwise stated, the opinions of the author only; they should not be inferred to be those of any other individual or organization.

ISBN: 978-1-4834-7809-8 (sc)
ISBN: 978-1-4834-7810-4 (hc)
ISBN: 978-1-4834-7802-9 (e)

Library of Congress Control Number: 2017914036

Because of the dynamic nature of the Internet, any web addresses or links contained in this book may have changed since publication and may no longer be valid. The views expressed in this work are solely those of the author and do not necessarily reflect the views of the publisher, and the publisher hereby disclaims any responsibility for them.

Cover design by Ferris Crane and Karlie Slutiak
Demonstrators: Kiryu Kimio and the author
Photography: Iguchi Wako

Lulu Publishing Services rev. date: 10/12/2017

Dedication

At the beginning of the twentieth century, after staying secret for unrecorded ages, Karate entered public schools and public *dōjō*. However, only the outer aspects of the art have been revealed – the outer movements – often without proper explanations of practical meaning. My intention is to explain those secrets.

Faced with a centuries-long silence, I hesitated to publicly disclose the meanings of Kata movements. After all, no one to my knowledge had done it before. After long soul-searching, however, I decided that I have not only the right but the obligation to so for the sake of advancing the art. I pray that the spirits of *Budō* will not be jealous.

I dedicate this book to the memory of the venerable Sugiyama Shojiro-sensei, my favorite teacher, who inspired his students to surpass his own level of accomplishments. He will be forever missed. I hope that my humble attempts to elucidate the hidden meanings of Kata movements will meet with his approval from his place of eternal rest.

CALLIGRAPHY BY SUGIYAMA SHOJIRO-SENSEI
DEPICTING PHONETIC REPRESENTATION
OF THE AUTHOR'S NAME IN KANJI

Words of Thanks

Thinking "What could be easier than writing a book about Karate?," I readily plunged into the project, only to discover I could not complete it all alone.

For starters, I needed a partner to practice Kata movements, someone willing to spend with me several hours a week for a number of consecutive months. Luckily, one day I ran into a *senpai* of mine with 50 years of Karate under his belt – Kiryu Kimio, who unhesitatingly agreed to support me in my writing venture. Asking nothing in return, his unstinting contribution has been a pure labor of love, with "no expectations" as he put it. Luckily, over the years, Kiryu *senpai* had complemented his Karate with Aikido practice, which proved a tremendous advantage to demonstrating the throwing techniques I wanted to present in the book. Thank you, Kiryu *senpai*!

Also, I needed someone to photograph my interpretation of Kata movements. Luckily, I found out that Ms. Iguchi Wako, with whom I used to practice Karate, was a professional photographer. No sooner had I asked than she willingly took the initiative for every detail of the photography. It was a joy to see a professional photographer in action. Thank you, Iguchi san! (Ms. Iguchi's e-mail address is: wako.workshop@gmail.com and her Instagram username is: wakoiguchi)

In another stroke of good luck, Mr. Yamamoto Gonnohyōe, 10th Dan and Chairman of the International Karate-Do Organization (IKO) (http://www.iko-goju.com/eng/), allowed us to conduct photography sessions in his Tokyo *dōjō*, asking nothing in return. Thank you indeed!

Then, Patrick McCarthy, Hanshi 9th dan, a monumental figure in the world of Karate with accomplishments and contributions to martial arts beyond count, kindly agreed to review and write a foreword to the book, instilling me with an extra layer of confidence. Patrick-sensei is the director of the International Ryukyu Karate-jutsu Research Society (IRRS) (http://www.koryu-uchinadi.com/). Without his constructive comments, for which I am forever grateful, this book could not have been completed. Thank you, Patrick-sensei!

As the publishing deadline drew near, I realized that I needed someone to read the manuscript and point out grammar errors and lapses in clarity. Chris Pitts, a professor of English language and literature at a university in Tokyo, who has extensive editing experience, agreed to brush up the first draft. Thank you, Chris!

Another challenge: the book needed a design for its front and back cover, and the spine. A friend, artist and graphic designer, Ferris Crane of *Ferris Crane Communications Designs* (FCCD) and Robert Morris University, came through, as she always does, offering her professional services despite her heavy workload. Thank you, Ferris!

Finally, I asked my Karate friend, Yamamoto Kazuki, to check the kanji used in the text – a request to which he gladly agreed. Thank you, Yamamoto san!

There are many other people to whom I owe thanks; people who over the years have supported my passion for Karate. Thank you all!

Contents

Foreword

Karate is no longer taught as it used to be. As everything in life it moves forward with the changing times. But without linking the modern with the past, the timeless lessons of old may elude us. I've long believed that a link to the past is also a bridge to the future. The Japanese proverb, *On Ko Chi Shin* (温故知新), reminds us that, *By studying the old, we better understand the new.*

In many ways, the work that lies before you, *Black Belts Only,* exemplifies such a proverb in that it helps bring Karate to life – but not as sport, competition or self-defense. Rather, it brings Karate to life as *Budō* (武道), with its power to kill with one devastating single blow. Such power, however, carries heavy responsibility – the responsibility of never using it randomly and never for selfish reasons.

To develop such power, honing the focus of technique becomes imperative, and for Newhouse, repeated *maki-wara* practice is essential. His analysis of a perfect *maki-wara* strike misses nothing as he walks the reader step by step through the correct body and fist positions, breathing, muscle contraction and use of eyes.

The lethal power of *kime* (決め), however, has nothing to do with physical strength. For Newhouse the answer lies in mastering *Ki* energies circulating all around us, including our and our opponents' bodies. Instead of brute force, this author says, *"We apply the Eastern principles of In~Yo (Yin & Yang) in our training."* Resonating Master Funakoshi's sentiment, Newhouse explains, *"Only by becoming weak – by replacing physical strength with Ki (気) – can we become strong."*

But to awaken and foster *Ki* possessed of power, courage and resolve, we must first master ourselves, abandoning petty attachments and desires that block the flow of such energy. The idea of studying the ways of the samurai warriors, who grew in power as they preoccupied themselves with daily thoughts of death, subsequently becomes of great value in such a pursuit. Then, Newhouse says, the energies of ancient warriors will find a welcome abode within us.

We aim at benefiting society, says Newhouse, with benevolence toward all as our guiding principle. Limiting ourselves to Karate alone is not enough. We follow other passions along the noble dictates of *bunbu ryōdō* (文武両道) – combining physical with literary pursuits as a twin path. In such a pursuit it becomes possible for our skills to flourish and *Ki* to bloom.

Because, according to Newhouse, *Ki* energy is endowed with intelligence, we must teach it so that, when necessary, it will work of its own accord without our conscious involvement. Here lies the secret: mindless repetitions of movement will not advance our Karate. Unless performed mindfully, with full recognition of the underlying meaning, techniques – no matter how often repeated – will never mature.

True to his word, the author follows up by taking a fresh look at Kata, replacing centuries-old accumulated "nonsense" with new original meaning, recognizing patterns, and discovering hidden universal conventions. Suddenly, what looks like a "punch" acquires a different meaning; what looks like a "block" finds a new application. The result is a comprehensive system of Kata interpretation based on methods of escape as originally advanced in the time-honored text, *Bubishi* – the "bible" of Karate.

I welcome this work into my library and believe that it will enrich the thinking and practice of every serious student of Karate. Linking the past with the present can help bring together like-minded people in pursuit of common goals and celebrate empowerment, personal achievement and camaraderie through this ancient art. I believe the work that lies before you makes such a link, resurrecting what has been forgotten and misrepresented and seamlessly tying it to the practice of today. In doing so, *Black Belts Only* provides new and deeper meaning to aspects of Karate that have fallen quietly dormant in modern times. I highly recommend this work by Adam Newhouse.

Patrick McCarthy
Hanshi 9th Dan
Director
International Ryukyu Karate-jutsu Research Society

Preface

*The flower of Karate that blossomed in Ryūkyū, having spread far
and wide throughout our country [Japan], has borne fruit and will,
I believe, contribute to launching the Japanese people onto the world
stage.*[1]

—Master Funakoshi Gichin

Entering my first Karate *dōjō* almost forty years ago, I searched in vain for
books to help me understand Kata movements. Some books' explanations
made little sense. Other books gave instructions such as "assume the position shown in the adjacent photograph." Not much different from what
I found in the pioneering 1925 *Karate Jutsu* by Master Funakoshi Gichin.
Not exactly what I was looking for.

Over the next forty years, I asked and studied, tried and erred. I practiced in many *dōjō* under many instructors, sometimes several times a
day. Traveling, I packed my Karate uniform (*dō-gi*) in my bag and visited
local training halls. Even on my honeymoon, I found myself practicing
away from home ... sporting a new wedding ring. To my surprise, I was
curtly told that wedding rings were a no-no in a *dōjō*. It just never had
occurred to me.

More important: I never stopped asking questions.

I watch people entering *dōjō* for the first time. Some ask a question
or two to satisfy their initial thirst to discover the meaning of it all. Not
for long. By the time they earn their brown or black belts, their curiosity
disappears. They just go through the motions of *kihon*, Kata and *kumite*
practice, believing they already know it all. If they initially received some
explanations they never investigated their validity. Now they dogmati-
cally follow what they were told. If they see something new, they may
say "so what?"

With the richness and largely unexplored mysteries and depths
of Karate, their attitude is puzzling. Learning Karate is like learning

---

[1] Master Funakoshi Gichin, *The Essence of Karate* 103 (Richard Berger trans., Kodansha
2013) (*"Essence"*).

a foreign language. Without understanding the meaning of words, it would be foolhardy to claim mastery. I once asked a friend to explain the meaning of an English phrase he was fond of using. He said that he didn't know the meaning but his father often used that expression and the clients liked it. I wish that our attitude to Karate were a little more mature.

This book is meant to change this state of things by offering serious students of Karate of all levels a novel way to interpret Kata. As far as I know, most explanations and most conventions employed in the Kata that I describe are new.

My purpose is to offer an alternate way of looking at Karate and its Kata to those who still look for answers. Some may regard the theories and ideas presented as coming out of left field – strange and irrelevant. In the context of the teaching philosophies of Karate today this is to be expected. You, the reader, are free to accept any of the explanations or reject them as you wish.

Lest I too become a victim of dogmatic thinking, let me stress that what I present is just *an* interpretation as I alone see it. It is not meant as *the* interpretation of Karate and its Kata techniques, which have many alternative meanings and variations. Indeed, analyzing the opening move of *Heian Go-dan* Kata alone, my mind was turning up a multiplicity of possible applications to the point that writing a manageable guidebook like this would be virtually impossible. Was I going insane, I wondered?

If anything, this is just an attempt to reconstitute theories latent in *Budō* Karate and make better sense of its Kata movements. Many concepts and techniques need further refinement and research. I encourage the reader to improve on them, experiment and seek alternative meanings.

For almost a century since its introduction to Japan, with a few notable exceptions such as the contributions by the venerable Sugiyama-sensei, Karate has not progressed an inch – it has regressed by miles. As Karate is soon to enter upon the Olympic stage, it is my hope that more people will begin to ask questions and find new answers. It's time to start thinking outside the box. They say that when a student is ready, the teacher will appear. I believe that we are all ready.

Tokyo, September 18, 2017

We Know the "How;" Now We Need the "Why"

If you stop here [and do not innovate], the glorious tradition will become a simple past.[2]

—Sugiyama Shojiro-sensei

With our bookshelves sagging under the weight of existing Karate books and YouTube offering a phantasmagoria of ever-newer video explanations of techniques, why yet another Karate book? Because book after book, video after video typically show us only the "how" of Karate. There is no "why" there.

This book goes into the "why." The new interpretations of techniques found here merely set a background to reach deeper into Karate and its philosophy – a philosophy of *Budō* to which Master Funakoshi Gichin elevated Karate from an obscure Okinawan system of fighting arts. The prism of "why" reveals that Karate techniques are merely physical manifestations of the spirit and mindset of ancient warriors.

We need the "why" to make sure that our Karate technique is not only sound, but is also aligned with its goals and mission. Indeed, the "why" will often change the "how" of our practice and redefine our relations with partners and other people.

This book introduces Karate as never before. It is not the Karate you will find in a local *dōjō*. It is based on new analytical concepts and methodologies, amply drawing on the teachings of traditional *Budō* and awash with the underlying philosophies of the East. The "newness" may indeed challenge our current understandings and expectations to the point that the experience may be transformational in nature.

Yet, this book is just the beginning. With each day, we learn new lessons and fathom new meanings. There is always more to learn.

I wrote this book for you:

---

[2] Sugiyama Shojiro-sensei, *11 Innovations in Karate* 8 (Version 2005) ("*11 Innovations*"); in Japanese the epigraph reads, "伝統も留まってしまえばただの過去."

- To tell you the why of Karate and explain why its secrets are still veiled in mystery;
- To give you for the first time both the practical and underlying meaning of many Kata techniques, including all Kata opening movements;
- To share with you secret conventions contained in the Kata;
- To inflame your passion and ignite your curiosity to explore the depths of Karate by probing beyond outer manifestations of form;
- To encourage you to question what you already know and fearlessly seek new meanings of techniques beyond their current textbook explanations;
- To suggest directions for self-study, since teachers only show the direction but the responsibility for reaching the destination is ours;
- To instill in you the value of self-teaching, since most Karate greats have been self-taught (if we want to reach high levels of Karate we must be our own teachers);
- To move you away from thinking of Karate as a fighting art or sport where scoring points becomes the highest goal or achievement;
- To broaden your inquiry by assimilating the concepts of Yin and Yang and *Ki* energy into Karate training;
- To ingrain in you the virtues of *Budō* of always seeking the best in yourself and being second to none; and
- To make your Karate practice all-encompassing, spilling over into all aspects of your life and endeavors.

****

"Why" has been Karate's taboo word, shunned and feared for too long. As a result, I believe that we have strayed from the original way. It's time to hit the reset button and boldly ask the question.

CHAPTER 1
Karate as *Budō*

The essential purpose of studying Karate is to learn how to coordinate all possible power in order to be able to finish an opponent with one blow. A sure finish with one blow is called ICHI-GEKI HISSATSU. Without this Karate does not exist.[3]

—Sugiyama Shojiro

Secrets of Budō Karate Revealed could be a more suitable title for this book. With the spread and popularity of Karate as a sport, however, Karate practitioners might find the notion of *Budō* Karate puzzling. Indeed, the essence of Karate as *Budō* lies in the development of the power to kill with one and only one technique, and "anything that lacks the power to kill a person [should the need ever arise to call upon such skills] could not be called a martial art."[4] But in today's societies, the idea of killing the opponent with one blow may seem irrelevant, uncivilized and out of date.

It's Not About Fighting

The ultimate aim of Karate lies not in victory nor defeat, but in the perfection of the character of its participants.[5]

—Master Funakoshi Gichin

If we have no power to kill with one blow we are likely doing something other than traditional Karate. But the ability to strike a mortal blow is far from what Karate is about. The goal of Karate is to become so strong that we simply cannot fight and won't fight. Indeed, becoming a target

---

[3] Sugiyama Shojiro-sensei, 1 *Kitoh Karate* 11 (1994).

[4] Master Funakoshi, *Essense* (cited in note 1) at 57.

[5] Master Funakoshi Gichin, quoted on the front flap of the jacket of his *The Twenty Guiding Principles of Karate: The Spiritual Legacy of the Master* (preface by Genwa Nakasone) (John Teramoto trans., Kodansha 2003) (*"Twenty Guiding Principles"*).

of an attack discloses some weakness or opening in our minds as Master Funakoshi pointed out.[6] The attacker is merely exploiting such weakness as should be obvious to those versed in the principles of Ying and Yang. To the extent that we expose such an opening, we attract the attack.

Quite divorced from the obsession with fighting and winning, the essence of *Budō* is to stop fighting. Master Funakoshi Gichin explained that *"bu"* (武), the first character of *Budō*, meaning "martial," consists of two parts. The first part means "to stop" (止), and the second means "halberds," or "spears" (戈). In short, the mission of *Budō* is to stop fighting.[7]

The non-combative aspect of Karate puzzles sports Karate practitioners, many of whom train with the mindset of a fighter, not so different from a pro wrestler or kickboxer. Admittedly, many of them excel as effective fighters. Sadly, this mindset may keep them from entering the enchanting world of *Budō*.

In one of my former *dōjō*, a teacher mysteriously said to me: "I do not fight you." "What did he mean?" I kept thinking. Of course, the teacher – by far a better and stronger person than me – wouldn't fight me. What would be the point?

The experience stuck with me, revealing the fundamental principle of *Budō* Karate to avoid fighting. As Karate teachers of old stressed again and again, at least in one-on-one situations, fighting is a selfish endeavor that undermines the sanctity of the art. Master Funakoshi, for one, insisted that, except for *dōjō* sparring, "fighting of any kind [is] forbidden." At least in his *dōjō*, "anyone caught fighting would [have been] instantly expelled."[8]

In his *Twenty Guiding Principles of Karate*, Master Funakoshi further confirms that conviction by quoting his teacher Itosu Anko:

> … when it becomes necessary, one should not regret laying
> down one's life for the sake of lord or parents, courageously
> sacrificing oneself for the common good. But Karate [teaches

---

[6] *See* Master Funakoshi Gichin, *Karate-Dō Kyōhan: The Master Text* 234 (Ohshima Tsutomu-sensei trans., Kodansha 1973) (*"Kyōhan"*).

[7] *See* Master Funakoshi, *Twenty Guiding Principles* (cited in note 5) at 25.

[8] Master Funakoshi Gichin, quoted by Jotaro Takagi in *Afterword* to Master Funakoshi, *Twenty Guiding Principles* (cited in note 5) at 119 – 20.

that] the true meaning of this does not apply to fighting with an enemy one on one. Therefore, in the event that you are accosted by a thug or challenged by an aggressive troublemaker, you should try to avoid striking a mortal blow.[9]

Not convinced? Consider another passage from Master Itosu's unpublished work:

Karate is not intended as a method of physical exercise for individuals. Rather, it is intended to prepare you for the eventuality that you may have to risk your life for your **parents** or courageously serve the nation. It is absolutely not intended for use in a fight against a single attacker. Even if you should happen to come across a robber or someone who intended to hurt you, you must harbor no intention of striking them.[10]

Beyond Self-Defense

There are those who interpret [the expression "to transcend combat"] superficially and look down on Karate as a fighting art. The beginner should disregard such an interpretation and practice as if he were engaged in deadly combat. Karate-dō should be understood as an art in which life or death is the result of a single error.[11]

—Egami Shigeru-sensei

Self-Defense Is for Beginners

Similarly, we don't pursue the art of Karate as self-defense because fighting for our own rights is a selfish act. The goal of Karate is grander. If we must fight, we do so when values higher than our own protection are at stake. If anything, the goal of Karate is to fight against our own limitations and

---

[9] *Ibid.* 24.

[10] Master Itosu Anko, quoted in Chitose Tsuyoshi-sensei, *Kempo Karate-Do: Universal Art of Self-Defense* 110 (Christopher Johnston trans., Shindokan 2000) (originally published in 1957).

[11] Egami Shigeru-sensei, *The Heart of Karate-Dō* 53 (rev'd ed., Kodansha 2000).

desires. To quote the venerable Sugiyama-sensei, "Karate is a Japanese martial art (*Budō*), which was devised to overcome human weakness and limitations by bringing out hidden or unnoticed potential."[12]

There is a crucial difference between self-defense and Karate, Sugiyama-sensei explained. "When acting in self-defense, you are acting in your own interest. You, yourself, are the subject to be protected." However, "when practicing Karate as *Budō*, somebody else or something greater than yourself is the subject to be protected."[13]

Sometimes, if all else fails, of course we may have to defend ourselves. It's common sense. But, in such cases, let's be guided by Master Itosu's ethos that gave the assailants the benefit of the doubt: let's talk first to see if fighting can be avoided – after all, "[our assailants] may not be bad men at heart."[14]

I Love You, I Love You ... I Don't Love You

> One must have the spirit and vigor of a tiger or wolf. One should have the dignity of a valiant tiger.[15]
>
> —Master Funakoshi Gichin

Karate gives us many opportunities to practice Master Itosu's philosophy. Perhaps unexpectedly, by sending soft energies of love toward the opponent, our martial powers grow. The softness will neutralize and disarm the sting of many attacks.

On the other hand, a mental posture of imminent retaliation invites a challenge, precipitating a violent encounter. Worse, our intention to deliver a strike may create openings in our minds, inviting more skillful opponents to pounce upon them. If we call ourselves *Budō-ka*, we don't need to posture, threaten, or show off. We are not afraid. We keep our

---

[12] Sugiyama-sensei, *11 Innovations* (cited in note 2) at 10.

[13] *Ibid.*

[14] *See* Master Funakoshi Gichin, *Karate-Dō: My Way of Life* 50 (Kodansha 1975) ("*My Way of Life*").

[15] Master Funakoshi Gichin, *Karate Jutsu: The Original Teachings of Master Funakoshi* 176 (John Teramoto trans., Kodansha 2001) ("*Karate Jutsu*").

martial abilities hidden, like the skilled hawk in the Japanese proverb, which keeps its talons hidden.[16]

If the opponent nevertheless persists on hurting us, we can instantly withdraw the loving attribute of our nature. As the old saying goes, "A clenched fist should be like a hidden treasure up one's sleeve; it remains a secret until someone comes looking for it."[17]

Ideally, "[w]hen angered [we] can make even a ferocious beast crouch in fear, but when [we] smile even little children run to [us]."[18] The key is to master this transformation of love into all-out counterattack, suddenly and without hesitation turning soft energies into hard. As the venerable Sugiyama-sensei was fond of saying, we first show a mental posture of "I love you, I love you," sending energies of our big open heart toward our partners. But if our love is disrespected, we quickly reverse our attitude to "I no longer love you," by delivering a finishing blow.

Kumite Without Winners

Do not think of winning. Think, rather, of not losing.[19]
—Master Funakoshi Gichin
(His Twelfth Guiding Principle of Karate)

Kumite has always been part of Karate training. It has to be. Without practicing *kumite*, we might as well limit ourselves to reading books or watching martial arts movies. We need to internalize theories with our bodies and we cannot do it alone. Through sparring we put theory into practice, giving our bodies the freedom to learn. Yet, we must take care that our approach to *kumite* serves proper pedagogical purposes supporting the central values Karate is meant to foster.

---

[16] The original proverb says: *Nō aru taka tsume wo kakusu.*

[17] A saying quoted by Kyan Chōtoku-sensei in *Karate Training & What to Know About Fighting*, as recounted in Motobu Choki-sensei's 1932 *Watashi no Karate-jutsu (Karate My Art)* 48 (compiled and translated by Patrick & Yuriko McCarthy, International Ryukyu Karate Research Group 2002) ("*Watashi no Karate-jutsu*").

[18] Master Funakoshi, *Twenty Guiding Principles* (cited in note 5) at 71.

[19] *Ibid.*, 71.

Time to Grow Up

When we face an opponent, the space between us is filled with a blend of our mutual energies, often in a state of chaos. For some children such a state is unacceptable – they feel an irresistible urge to prove that their energies are stronger and initiate fights. One child subdues the other. A winner and a loser emerge. The order of things is restored.

As we grow up, such behavior may strike us as immature yet it is all around us – in business, on the street, and in sporting arenas.

The child's desire to determine who is "stronger" probably originates from feelings of insecurity. Later, however, unless eradicated in time, this childish impulse may produce individuals with rigid minds prone to bullying behavior. I believe that *Budō* Karate is a better way to prove our prowess by teaching respect of others and encouraging self-improvement.

Some people, however, never seem to get it. Years ago, a senior Karate practitioner already in his 60s entered a *kumite* competition for seniors. After losing a match, he commented: "I may have lost to him but I was much stronger than him." Go figure.

To Win or Not to Win: That Is the Question

Years ago, I noticed that more experienced or skillful practitioners would always do better than their partners in *kumite*. Instinctively, I felt that continuing this was helping no one. The stronger person might get arrogant and proud, the losing person might get placidly used to the idea of losing. Let us be more magnanimous and allow less experienced students to taste a moment of "winning" while we taste a sense of "losing" from time to time. As Shogun Tokugawa Ieyasu aptly put it, "Knowing only how to win and not how to lose is self-defeating."[20]

---

[20] Master Funakoshi, *Twenty Guiding Principles* (cited in note 5) at 71, quoting Shogun Tokugawa Ieyasu.

Seeking Unity with Others

On a higher level there is no winning or losing in Karate. These concepts may be OK for the uninitiated who, upon seeing a well-built man, may ask: "Can I take him on?" This way of thinking has nothing to do with *Budō* Karate, which is a sublime art devoid of notions of egotism or separation. As Chitose Tsuyoshi-sensei put it, *"Budō* is the stillness that results from discipline. It clears your soul and allows you to become one with nature."[21]

Just yesterday, on my way home from work, I noticed a young woman with a cute little dog on a long leash. They walked side by side about two yards apart. Suddenly, a bicycle came speeding from behind, tearing into the leash. It was already dark and the cyclist probably didn't notice the leash or the dog. The little dog was bruised and shaken, while the poor woman screamed, seeing it brutally yanked out of its leisurely stroll.

On reflection, I thought that, despite the leash, there was no real connection between the woman and the dog. The leash was actually loosely touching the surface of the road. Even though they walked not so far from each other, they were like two separate items. There was no unity between them. No wonder the cyclist could not sense that they were walking together. On top of that, the woman was fixated on her mobile device at the time. (As we'll see later, by doing so, she put herself in a vulnerable condition of *kyo*.)

When we face an opponent, we don't want to be like that woman with the dog. We want to be connected to the opponent; to instantly adjust to their every mental and physical action. We want an invisible leash always tightly stretched between us.

In his *Heart of Karate-Dō*, Egami Shigeru-sensei talks about pursuing unity with the opponent. Upon reaching such a state of mind, he continues, notions of winning and losing give way to notions of coexistence, harmony and cooperation.[22] Splendid, but how do we reach such an elevated state of mind?

Thinking kindly of the opponent may be a stepping stone to acquiring

---

[21] Chitose-sensei (cited in note 10) at 19.

[22] *See* Egami-sensei (cited in note 11) at 15.

this holistic spirit. Further along the way, we need to purify our minds of mundane desires, emptying our hearts and souls. We need to purge them of fear, greed, pride or ambition; from grudges, resentments and petty peeves. In the end, there will be no self and no opponent.[23]

Engaging in regular practice of pre-arranged and free *kumite* in the spirit of seeking unity with our partners will help us attain these higher spiritual grounds of *Budō*. Constantly probing and exchanging mutual energies is essential. Fusing our energies with our partners will help us to instantly read their feints and intentions to attack. Feeling their energies, we'll be able to react with a sense of unity without a single thought on our part.

In these days of group practice, opportunities to engage in pre-arranged sparring abound during every *keiko* (practice). I believe that we should take advantage of it by giving students more opportunities to learn and experiment how to handle the energies of different partners.

If we want to unite with them and naturally sense their movements and feel their breathing, thinking in terms of winning and losing makes no sense. Winning implies separation from the opponent. As such, it is incompatible with what true Karate is about.

The Last Opponent

"When one steps out of the carriage, one is among the dead; when one steps out of the door, the enemy is waiting." The point is not that one has to be careful, but that before one steps out, one has to already be dead.[24]

—Yamamoto Tsunetomo

Finding Emptiness

One thing that may prevent us from achieving true unity with our partners or attackers is our egos. The last opponent is us. There is no other.

[23] *See* Jotaro Takagi in his *Afterword* to Master Funakoshi, *Twenty Guiding Principles* (cited in note5) at 120.
[24] Yamamoto Tsunetomo, *The Art of the Samurai: Yamamoto Tsunetomo's Hagakure* 240 (Barry D. Steben trans., Duncan Baird 2008).

Our mission in relentlessly pursuing The Way of *Budō* is to dispose of this opponent. It is our true enemy. Let's get him out of our minds. Let's transcend our mortal reality.

We tend to quickly notice when another person is rude or unkind to us but often don't recognize when that other is no one else but us. It's time to take on this elusive enemy. If we don't, our attachment to desires and ideas will obscure our vision of reality and blur the clarity of our minds. I believe that changing the name of Karate to "Empty Hands" is emblematic of this concept of emptying our hearts and minds. As Master Funakoshi reminded us, "the form of the universe is emptiness and emptiness is form," or *"shiki-soku-ze-kū, kū-soku-ze-shiki."*[25]

Dying Every Day

I have found that <u>bushidō</u> means to die. … If every morning and every evening one dies anew, one will become as one who is permanently dead. Thus will one obtain a real freedom in <u>bushidō</u> ….[26]
—Yamamoto Tsunetomo

The Way of *Budō* leads to eradicating the concept of self on a daily basis by facing and experiencing death, whether mentally or on a battlefield. As long as we live, we have attachments and desires – things that make us weak. By facing death, our attachments suddenly disappear, transporting us to a land of absolute freedom – freedom from ourselves.

Ohshima Tsutomu-sensei points out that *Budō* begins by "cutting ourselves" – *onore wo kiru*. "In *Budō*," he continues, "we realize that one's true opponent is oneself, and in constantly trying to imagine ourselves in the face of death, we seek to forge, harden and discipline our minds and bodies."[27]

When we deny our existence, clearing our minds of selfish distractions, we enter a world where making decisions and taking action to

---

[25] *See, e.g.,* Master Funakoshi, *My Way of Life* (cited in note 14) at 35; Master Funakoshi, *Kyōhan* (cited in note 6) at 4.

[26] Yamamoto (cited in note 24) at 43 – 44.

[27] Ohshima Tsutomu-sensei, *Notes on Training* 237 (Pine Wind Press 1998) (*"Notes on Training"*).

defend honor and justice is easy, as notions of survival no longer cloud our thinking. Indeed, striving to reach a state of mind attached to neither this nor the other world is truly The Way of *Budō*.

Attaining mastery in *Budō* was unimaginable for an ancient samurai without a consuming contemplation of death. Death was his daily preoccupation. Each morning, after rising and "pacifying [his] body and mind" he was to visualize being "chopped into pieces by bows and arrows, muskets, a spear or a sword." He was to imagine himself "[having] been swept up by a gigantic wave," and "thrown into a great fire." He was to think of himself being "pulverized by a bolt of lightning" and "violently shaken by a great earthquake." He was to see himself "jumping off a precipitous cliff" and having "just died of illness or suddenly dropped dead."[28] He was to reach a state of mind of actually being dead.

A Story of Instant *Budō* Mastery

One day a young samurai appeared before Chiba Shūsaku – one of the greatest samurai who ever lived (considered to be one of the "last saints of the sword" or *ken-sei*[29]) – saying that he had been waylaid by a *tsuji-giri*[30] who apparently wanted to test his new sword on him.[31] The young samurai, realizing the formidable strength of the *tsujigiri*, pleaded to let him complete an errand for his lord, promising to return. Having little confidence in his ability and not wanting to die a cowardly death – for he had no illusions of surviving the duel – the young samurai sought Shūsaku's advice on how to die honorably, confessing that he had already resolved to die.

Shūsaku suggested that during the encounter the young samurai

---

[28] *See* Yamamoto (cited in note 24) at 240.

[29] Not to be mistaken with *ken-sei* (拳聖) denoting "saints of the fist," or "fist saints" – an honorific title awarded to a few masters of Karate (including Master Itosu Anko and Master Kanryo Higaonna), which uses the Chinese character *ken* (拳) meaning fist rather than *ken* (劍) meaning sword.

[30] *Tsujigiri* (literally "crossroads cut[ter]") were samurai who would waylay random strangers in order to test their new weapons or skills; the practice is also referred to as *tsujigiri*. *See* https://en.wikipedia.org/wiki/Tsujigiri

[31] The story as recounted by Sugiyama Shojiro-sensei in his *11 Innovations* (cited in note 2) at 264.

hold his sword high above his head, close his eyes and imagine himself already dead in the other world. Upon returning to meet the *tsujigiri*, the young samurai did as Shūsaku advised. Seeing that, the *tsujigiri* was dumbfounded. He knew he could easily kill the young man but the possibility of the suspended sword falling on him at the moment of a strike him gave him a pause. They faced each other for a long time, during which the young samurai never changed his pose. In the end, exclaiming "Excellent," the *tsujigiri* quickly went away.

Shūsaku had sent one of his students to secretly watch the encounter, and, on hearing the report, commented:

> The young samurai did not intend to live any longer in this
> world, so he could reach in one second the state of mind which
> sword masters spend their entire lives trying to reach.[32]

The story contains points to ponder for all *Karate-ka* who study their art seriously. It resonates well with Master Funakoshi's teachings that mastery of Karate equals mastery over ourselves.

---

[32] *Ibid.*

CHAPTER 2

Karate as Sport

In the old days we trained Karate as a martial art, but now they train
Karate as a gymnastic sport. I think we must avoid treating Karate
as a sport – it must be a martial art at all times! Your fingers and the
tips of your toes must be like arrows, your arms must be like iron. You
have to think that if you kick, you try to kick the enemy dead. If you
punch, you must thrust to kill. If you strike, then you strike to kill the
enemy. This is the spirit you need in order to progress in your training.
—Choshin Chibana-sensei

Ending the Secrecy: Karate's Denobling Days

Karate reached Okinawan shores before weapons were banned on the
Ryūkyū Islands. In 1392, thirty-six families from Fujian province in
China, including teachers of Chinese martial arts, arrived and established
a community in Naha as part of a cultural exchange.[33] The Okinawans'
love affair with "Chinese hands" or "Tang Hands" (the meaning of the
orginal kanji of Karate) had begun.

However, the ban on weapons in 1477 by King Shō Shin following
the reunification of Okinawa and the creation of the Ryūkyū Kingdom
by King Shō Hashi in 1429 may have added an impetus to study and learn
Chinese hand fighting techniques.[34] With the reinstitution of the ban by
the invading forces of the Satsuma clan, which seized the Kingdom in
1609, weaponless fighting arts kept forging their way into mainstream
Okinawan culture. So much so that, by the Meiji Restoration, the newly
established Meiji government viewed Karate as a threat and simply pro-
hibited its teaching. As Master Funakoshi recalls, during his younger days

---

[33] *See* https://en.wikipedia.org/wiki/Karate#Okinawa

[34] *Ibid.*

"the practice of Karate was banned by the government." Instruction took place at night, and talking about Karate was strictly forbidden.[35]

Then suddenly, after ages of secrecy, Karate gained its freedom of expression, ending up on public school curriculums. The passage from secrecy into the limelight coincided with the rise of military spirit in Japan. If the Okinawan weaponless arts stressed restraint and condemned senseless fighting, under the new regime, brute force began to replace their original noble spirit.

The emphasis now turned mainly to building strong physiques. The notion was that, in comparison to other people, Karate practitioners looked stronger and healthier.[36] This perspective probably initiated a gradual departure of Karate from the land of *Budō* into the land of sports and physical exercise.

A Fighting Art

I do recall, however, that when I visited Okinawa in 1940, I saw no sparring; in fact, I heard that some karateka were ousted from their dōjō because they had adopted sparring after having learned it in Tokyo.[37]

—Egami Shigeru-sensei

Perversely perhaps, and in contrast to the principles of *Budō*, today's sports Karate appears to encourage fighting, as winning tournaments brings instant group recognition and awards. (Think of the trophies and framed photos of bemedalled competition winners prominently displayed in a typical Karate club.) In so many *dōjō*, the day of a tournament resembles a national holiday: their doors close as practitioners assemble in the fighting arena to win matches and earn coveted trophies. For many, competitive *jiyū kumite* has become the be-all-and-end-all of Karate. What matters is scoring points.

If old masters built high fences to prevent onlookers from peeking

---

[35] Master Funakoshi, *My Way of Life* (cited in note 14) at 4.
[36] *See* Master Funakoshi, *Karate Jutsu* (cited in note 15) at 28.
[37] Egami-sensei (cited in note 11) at 113.

in, today we delight in watching public Karate performances. Spectacular feats of *Karate-ka* executing defensive and offensive techniques against multiple opponents fascinate us. Breaking boards and making unnecessary noises to achieve special effects are par for the course.

"The usual exchange of blows in the *dōjō*," however, "is not *Budō* – it is sport," as Chitose Tsuyoshi-sensei of *Chitō-ryū* fame reflected.[38]

Sadly, the macho aura oozing from today's halls of practice encourages members to get into a fight at the slightest provocation. But, as Master Funakoshi pointed out, "an ordinary man [who draws] his sword when ridiculed and [fights] risking his life," is not "a courageous man." Rather, "a truly great man is not disturbed even when suddenly confronted with an unexpected event or crisis." Such a man is beyond ego-centered pride and petty revenge "because he has a great heart and his aim is high."[39]

Those who say that we cannot progress in Karate without engaging in actual fights, or, if we cannot overpower a certain person, we might as well quit Karate right there and then, have little knowledge of what Karate-dō is about. Their attitude is "truly grievous [to its reputation]."[40]

I never understood why some people who equate Karate with fighting don't take up boxing instead – a discipline that doesn't make any pretences and probably offers a better fighting regimen. I believe that the allure of *Budō* spirit may be the main attraction. But then, they get caught up in the fighting mentality of today's practice, forgetting their original dream. Yet, *Budō* spirit is still there. We just need to find it.

Feel-Good Exercises

> *Karate is not simply a game. If there are those who understand Karate to be a pastime for men of leisure or a performance put on just for spectators, then this is a folly similar to hastily confusing the swordplay in stage and cinema for the secrets of the martial arts.*[41]
>
> —Chitose Tsuyoshi-sensei

---

[38] Chitose-sensei (cited in note 10) at 19.

[39] *See* Master Funakoshi, *Kyōhan* (cited in note 6) at 248

[40] *See ibid*, 5.

[41] Chitose-sensei (cited in note 10) at 91.

A TV interview with a Kendo practitioner captured my attention. The person praised Kendo for helping her relax after a busy day, and for keeping her in good shape. At another time, a relative asked me what I did in my free time. Hearing about Karate, she suggested that, in addition to engaging in such a selfish pursuit – benefiting nobody but myself – I might also think of doing something to benefit others. Indeed, the notion that we pursue martial arts for pleasure or other selfish gains is common.

But don't get me wrong. I have nothing against practicing Karate as a sport. Indeed, I often infuse elements of fun to my Karate training and at some point may have practiced it as a form of physical exercise while enjoying friendly *kumite* bouts. I believe that, especially these days, we can enhance learning by combining our practice with a dose of playfulness and fun. A measure of competition may also contribute to quicker progress. If practicing Karate as a form of physical exercise in a spirit of friendly competition can benefit our health and increase our happiness, I have no problem with it. Except:

Sun-Dome Honored in the Breach

> You should never raise your hand against your opponent first. Only when it becomes absolutely necessary should you raise your hand. And even then, your intention should not be to kill or injure your opponent but only to block his attack. If he continues, then you should take a stance that will clearly show that it would be best for him to stop.[42]
> —Master Funakoshi Gichin

With its overarching concern of not hurting the opponent, the unselfish aspects of *Budō* seem irreconcilable with today's preoccupation with scoring points. Either we "hold as an essential principle that avoidance of injury to others with [our] fists and feet is [our] first concern"[43] as Master

---

[42] Master Funakoshi Gichin, quoted in Egami (cited in note 11) at 15.

[43] *See* Master Itosu Anko, quoted in *Twenty Guiding Principles* (cited in note 5) at 24.

Itosu instructed, or we covet winning tournament trophies – there is no middle ground.[44]

Losing a Friend

> *In legal disputes or arguments, there are times when one loses quickly and when it is most admirable to lose. It is just like it is in sumo wrestling. To be in a hurry just to win and end up winning in a dirty way is worse than losing.*[45]

—Yamamoto Tsunetomo

The principle of *sun-dome*, or stopping a strike just short of a target, appears to be open to practitioners' interpretation. All too often it is observed in the breach – intentionally or otherwise, but small comfort to the person on the receiving end. Actually, to some Karate veterans, signs of former injuries present an opportunity for tacit or overt pride: "In the old days, we used to ...."

Kumite in the spirit of learning and testing one's skills and techniques is one thing. *Kumite* in the spirit of winning at all costs is another. In today's Karate culture, losing means loss of reputation – nobody feels for the loser, everyone sides with the winner. Goaded by peers, spurred by pride, and even egged on by instructors, sparring partners sometimes lose control. They want to prove themselves in front of others. "Friendly" sparring turns into a dogfight. Injuries follow.

To be fair, injuries are mostly unintentional. Yes, we drum into students' minds that controlling attacks is sacrosanct, especially in case of more experienced practitioners. Otherwise, without implicitly trusting each other, practicing *kumite* is pointless and self-defeating. But even after years of practice, our bodies will sometimes react involuntarily – this should be expected. On the other hand, over the years, I've seen many

---

[44] Compare Master Funakoshi' view in his 1925 *Karate Jutsu* that "The reason that until now there has been no assigning of ranks in Karate is that it has not been possible to have *shiai* (competitive matches) as in *jūdō* or *kendō*. This is because of the devastating power of Karate techniques; a strike to a vital point could immediately prove fatal." Master Funakoshi, *Karate Jutsu* (cited in note 15) at 27.

[45] Yamamoto (cited in note 24) at 103.

mean-spirited people in a *dōjō* who just like to hurt others. Instructors often turn a blind eye, tacitly condoning such behavior. The answer: let's always be prepared, not giving our partners any benefit of the doubt. Let's always be on guard. Accidents will happen.

Years ago, in my youthful zeal for the art, I recommended Karate to a good friend of mine. Later, during *kumite*, things took a somewhat personal and ugly turn: my friend suffered an internal injury because of a vicious punch to his body. As a result, I lost a friend. With hindsight, I see that I should never have recommended Karate to my friend – at least not as it is practiced in some *dōjō* today.

Bullies in a *Dōjō*

> Rei *is often defined as "respect," but it actually means much more. …*
> *It is said that "without* rei *there is disorder," and also that "the difference between men and animals lies in* rei*." Combat methods that lack* rei *are not martial arts but merely contemptible violence. Physical power without* rei *is no more than brute strength, and for human beings it is without value.*[46]
>
> —Master Funakoshi Gichin

Beating up on or showing no respect to other students is irreconcilable with the spirit of Karate. I sometimes observe practitioners who believe that they are commanders of correctional facilities whose role is to terrorize inmates into submission and obedience. I also see people who do not seem to mind hurting others during *kumite*. They say Karate is "*Budō*," and if someone gets hurt it's an unintended but necessary part of it. On occasion, even an instructor may behave that way while sparring with a student. As a result, less advanced students lose heart, becoming disenchanted with the art.

On the way to mastery, at any given time, different students are on different levels of development. Some may be way ahead, some far behind. Karate practice should encourage all students to make steady progress.

---

[46] Master Funakoshi, *Twenty Guiding Principles* (cited in note 5) at 19 – 20.

Many of the past Karate heavyweights began practicing as self-admitted weaklings. Gradually, with training, their weaknesses metamorphosed into spectacular strengths. If Karate were only for the strong, it would probably never have been born. Unfortunately, bullying in *dōjō* is not uncommon. It is a crime against the spirit and dignity of *Budō*. Sadly, it stops many practitioners along The Way.

You Don't Teach Here

Tigress:	*You don't belong here.*
Kung Fu Panda:	*Uh, yeah, yeah. Of course. This is your room.*
Tigress:	*I mean … you don't belong in the Jade Palace. You're a disgrace to Kung Fu, and if you have any respect for who we are and what we do, you will be gone by morning.*[47]

In my youth when visiting various *dōjō* during my travels away from home, I sometimes couldn't resist sharing with others what I had learned. Suddenly someone would approach me with a stern warning: "You don't teach here." I met with similar reactions even in *dōjō* to which I formally belonged. Apparently, my "teaching" or showing new techniques was too much for some self-appointed guardians of *dōjō* etiquette who felt compelled to give me the familiar *aisatsu* (greeting): "You don't teach here."

I should have known better. Often old-timers of a Karate club feel threatened by introductions of new methods, techniques or teaching philosophies. My meddling into their familiar ways apparently endangered the sanctity of their turf. Then again, my ideas may have been half-baked or perhaps taken from "other styles" of Karate, making things even worse. Still, the rebuffs rankled at the time.

The prevailing culture in today's *dōjō* rarely encourages free exploration of ancient teachings of *Budō*. Dialogue is not on the menu. And so we repeat largely meaningless motions, deluding ourselves that somehow the meaning will one day spontaneously appear.

---

[47] *Kung Fu Panda*, directed by John Stevenson and Mark Osborne, screenplay by Jonathan Aibel and Glenn Berger (DreamWorks Animation 2008).

Luckily, the Internet environment is challenging the rigidity of the old system. Young practitioners empowered by the emerging freedom to express themselves online are gradually opening the doors to ancient secrets to which many YouTube Karate presentations amply attest. Most encouraging!

Returning to the Roots

> *While Karate is not something that can be easily conveyed and is difficult to explain without presenting an actual demonstration, a characteristic that distinguishes it as Karate is that it cannot be commercialized or adapted for competition. Herein lies the essence of Karate-dō, as it cannot be realized with protective equipment or through competitive matches.*[48]
>
> —Master Funakoshi Gichin

Alas, most YouTube demonstrations of *bunkai* (applications of techniques) are colored by the spirit of fighting and *kumite*. The unwritten goal of Karate in the minds of many people today is to subdue the opponent by inflicting injury. Once the official message that sparring is not only perfectly acceptable but indeed encouraged has captured their minds, they will continue to be mesmerized by it.

Unfortunately, if we hold on to the notion of Karate as a fighting art, I don't think we'll ever uncover the ancient meanings hidden in Kata. We simply won't know what to look for. If, on the other hand, we take to heart the precepts of old masters that Karate is not, barring special circumstances, meant as a weapon against a single opponent, those meanings are likely to spring to life for us spontaneously.

To revive the spirit of Karate we must consciously study the original meaning and application of techniques. Why not imitate Motobu Choki-sensei who would break into a sweat just thinking about performing a Kata, even when he was sitting.[49] Truly, his passion for analyzing and dissecting orthodox Kata movements was unparalleled.

---

[48] Master Funakoshi, *Essence* (cited in note 1) at 102.
[49] *See* Motobu-sensei, *Watashi no Karate-jutsu* (cited in note 17) at 31.

As Motobu-sensei reminded us, we don't learn only through our bodies, even if this may be the prevailing culture in today's *dōjō*. Recalling his earlier experiences, he tells us how his renowned teacher, Matsumora Kosaku, "[taught] his students how to think about what they were studying in order to develop and improve its application." Not surprisingly, "those who were unable to learn to think remained stiff and inflexible."[50]

Sadly, some former *Karate-ka* with whom I used to practice have abandoned Karate for less contentious forms of martial arts that encourage students to think, search and explore. They have given up on Karate and its senseless competitiveness and censorship of genuine inquiry. I hope that quitting Karate is not the only way. I hope that the non-fighting spirit of Karate can and will be restored and flourish in the near future.

Let's become as strong as we can be but remember that "Karate-dō has always been regarded as the martial art of gentlemen."[51] Keeping our power inside, let's show others the gentle side of our disposition.

May we be "gentle and never menacing; close, yet never forward." May we "slay but never humiliate." May "no sign of indecency [be] found in [our abodes]." May our "nourishment [be] never heavy." May we "be broadminded and strong-willed."[52] May our Karate be a "thoroughly noble martial art (*Budō*)" once again.[53]

[50] *Ibid.*, 104.
[51] Master Funakoshi, *Twenty Guiding Principles* (cited in note 5) at 72.
[52] Master Funakoshi, *Kyōhan* (cited in note 6) at 247 – 48.
[53] *See ibid.*, 5.

CHAPTER 3

Karate as a Way of Life

> *Herein lies the essence of Karate. More important than technique [jutsu (術) in Japanese] is the path [dō (道)]. That is to say, progressing from the technical aspect of Karate to the path that Karate itself represents. That is why in Ryūkyū, although the word Karate-jutsu does not exist, the word Karate-dō is an established term.*[54]
>
> —Master Funakoshi Gichin

Developing Good Moral Character

> *If one seeks out its true meaning, there is probably no martial art that does not lead to the cultivation of mental and moral strength.*[55]
>
> —Master Funakoshi Gichin

Karate instructors often tell parents that their children's moral character – and even their grades in school – will improve if they practice Karate regularly. I used to wonder if this was actually the case. But then, in my early years of practice, I lacked sufficient understanding of the underlying concepts of Karate to thoroughly investigate such questions; my familiarity with the principles of *Ki* and Yin and Yang was based mainly on book knowledge.

In general, those Karate teachers are right. Properly conducted, Karate practice emphasizes constant projection of energy. Disciples become more positive and outgoing. As a result, students become more active and sociable. They become less selfish or self-centered, more giving and extrovert. They are geared for success not only in Karate but also in other endeavors.

The development of positive dispositions, however, is not the only

---

[54] Master Funakoshi, *Essence* (cited in note 1) at 68.
[55] Master Funakoshi, *Karate Jutsu* (cited in note 15) at 30.

aim of practice. Unless students have a good moral foundation, Karate practice may in fact produce undesirable results by encouraging and empowering bullying behavior, cruelty and intolerance. As Master Funakoshi observed, "if Karate-dō is followed correctly, it will polish the character, and one will uphold justice, but if used for evil purposes, it will corrupt society and be contrary to humanity."[56]

This is why in olden days Karate masters would refuse to teach unless students came with superb recommendations stressing their good moral character. "Presumptuous or conceited" persons were thought "not qualified to follow Karate-dō."[57] "Those whose natures were deemed inappropriate, even in the case of one's own child, were strictly forbidden from receiving training in the martial arts."[58]

Karate is not for everyone. Luckily, those prone to violence often quit soon after entering a *dōjō*. If not, their arrogance and disrespect of others may only intensify, poisoning the atmosphere of an entire group.

There are exceptions. Even though Karate practice is not meant for ruffians or individuals showing a violent streak, in some cases it may pacify violent natures, as many Karate instructors have recognized.[59] If someone repeatedly asks for instruction, regardless of their current disposition or temperament, giving them a chance could lead to transformation of their character.

The remarkable turnaround of Motobu Choki-sensei – from a wild and boisterous youth, known to test his fighting prowess in haphazard brawls, to a restrained and respectable Karate teacher – attests to Karate's power not only to turn weaklings into formidable martial artists but also to pacify and control the violent streak of our natures.

To realize this potential – of reforming bullies into martial saints – our *dōjō* must cultivate high moral sense as their primary mission. Because *dōjō* doors are wide open, we must do all we can to preserve the high reputation of this wondrous art within society. We owe this much to all the Karate pioneers who came before us.

[56] Master Funakoshi, *Kyōhan* (cited in note 6) at 247.
[57] *Ibid.*, 6.
[58] Master Funakoshi, *Essence* (cited in note 1) at 69.
[59] *See, e.g., ibid.*, 70.

Humility and Dignity Without Ferocity or Servility

The first purpose in pursuing this art is the nurturing of a sublime spirit, a spirit of humility.[60]

—Master Funakoshi Gichin

What better way to achieve the *Budō's* ideal of avoiding confrontations than by practicing the virtue of humility in everything we do? Unexpressed passions, desires and emotions ennoble our hearts, and concealing them "should penetrate into all of [our] basic attitudes."[61]

If someone blocks our path, why not step aside without forcing a showdown? If someone insults us, why not ignore it? Even if someone hits us without causing us much harm, why not follow Master Itosu's advice and forgive, taking the incident in our stride?[62]

If we perceive gross injustice, however, we may have to act. We may even have to take the initiative. This too is part of *Budō*. But it only applies "when faced with a situation so unbearable that one's ability to tolerate it (or put an end to it without confrontation) is exhausted."[63]

Our goal is to seek peace and harmony while avoiding strife and conflict. This does not mean that we should allow others to trample on us. We should never be servile. Rather, let's strive to maintain our dignity – dignity tempered with humility. For dignity resides in "humility and self-control." It is found in "calm composure." It is noticed "in speaking few words." It exudes from "correct etiquette" and "gravity of deportment." And, it dwells in "determination and sharp-sightedness."[64]

Let's take to heart the teachings of Master Funakoshi that:

> One must have dignity without ferocity. Martial arts must bring one to this height. It will not do to act recklessly to no purpose and cause trouble for others. Masters and saints may

---

[60] Master Funakoshi Gichin, quoted in 1 Nakayama Masatoshi, *Best Karate: Comprehensive* 9 (Kodansha 1977).

[61] *See* Yamamoto (cited in note 24) at 87.

[62] *See* Master Funakoshi, *Essence* (cited in note 1) at 50.

[63] Master Funakoshi, *Twenty Guiding Principles* (cited in note 5) at 26.

[64] Yamamoto (cited in note 24) at 96 – 97.

appear as simpletons. Those who are pretentious declare to the world that they are just novice scholars or [novice] martial artists.[65]

Master Funakoshi passionately paved the road of Karate with virtue and self-improvement. In his world there was little room for discord, haughtiness or petty thinking. Let's practice Karate in that spirit for the pursuit of harmony and respect. Let's study the lives of *Karate-ka* of old to glean how to lead better lives.

Bunbu Ryōdō

> … *the literary arts (文) and the martial arts (武) must go hand in hand, never to be separated.*[66]
>
> —Master Funakoshi Gichin

We must not limit Karate practice to the time spent in a *dōjō*. *Budō* is all-encompassing and inseparable from the rest of our lives. The more we progress the more our rising martial spirit seeks new fountains of expression in other arts. Having truly mastered one art, we "possess versatility in all arts."[67] The more we advance in Karate, the higher we can aim in our literary and other artistic pursuits.

An obvious question: If a *Karate-ka* has no interests outside of Karate, how does this reflect on their Karate level?

Bunbu Ryōdō is a Japanese phrase describing a dual path of literary and martial pursuits. To follow such a path is commendable. It would be a pity if we channeled all our energies into Karate alone. We might become one-dimensional and it might reflect poorly on our Karate accomplishments as well.

We don't need excuses. Consider that the notoriously modest financial circumstances of many Karate practitioners of old Okinawa did not stop them from following other interests. Master Itosu Anko was a great

---

[65] Master Funakoshi, *Kyōhan* (cited in note 6) at 247.
[66] Master Funakoshi, *Karate Jutsu* (cited at note 15), *Preface to the Original Edition* at 21.
[67] *See* Master Funakoshi, *Essence* (cited in note 1) at 51.

calligrapher and scholar of Chinese classics. Master Azato Anko was also an exceptional scholar. Master Funakoshi Gichin studied and taught classical Chinese and Japanese philosophies and had an avid interest in poetry. [He wrote under the pen name *Shōtō* (松濤) – meaning literally pine waves or waving pines, and indicating the sound of wind rustling through pine trees – hence the name *Shōtō-kan* (松濤館), the *House of Shōtō*.] More importantly, Master Funakoshi has bequeathed to us several volumes of writings on Karate. The weaving of scholastic endeavors into those masters' daily lives does not appear to have been coincidental to their Karate greatness.

I do not suggest that each of us become a Confucian scholar. All I suggest is that we never stop learning outside of a *dōjō* so that our Karate never plateaus, stagnates or degrades.

Karate Is for Life

> *If a person does not make a stand for himself once and for all, nothing much will come of him. … It doesn't matter if you are a lay person or a monk: if you see some fellow making himself useful as a domainal elder or councillor, or if you see some monk who has established his own line of followers, one should think: "This fellow is also a human being, not a ghost or a god. Thus there is absolutely no reason why I should be inferior to him. If there is someone whom I cannot surpass, I will cut my belly and die."*[68]
>
> —Yamamoto Tsunetomo

Entering Reality

Our practice never ends. Karate is for life. Yet, there is never tomorrow, there is only now – an everlasting now. It is a moment of truth. Nothing is more precious. Reaching this state of mind is a challenge. To talk about it is easy – but these are just words. Still, I believe that entering into this elusive space of now will help us find The Way of *Budō* (or any other Way).

I used to split time between now and that "crucial" moment sometime

---

[68] Yamamoto (cited at note 24) at 240 – 41.

in the future. Practicing Karate, I thought that my training was divorced from reality. In other areas of life, I looked at the present merely as a rehearsal for some illusion of a better future. This is a mistake.

Budō teaches that there is nothing outside the present moment. Now is "the real thing."[69] There are no second chances. "Right now is that crucial moment, and that crucial moment is now." Indeed, if we think "of them as two, [we] will never be in time for that crucial moment."[70] There is only now – all past and future are already there.

This is how we practice. If we execute *mae-geri* in this spirit, it is for real at this very moment and it will be real at any other moment we may need to use it. It is not merely "getting ready" or "getting prepared." Our practice is real. There is no other time.

Surpassing Ourselves

> When Heaven is about to confer an important office upon a man, it first embitters his heart in its purpose; it causes him to exert his bones and sinews; it makes his body suffer hunger; it inflicts upon him want and poverty and confounds his undertakings. In this way it stimulates his will, steels his nature and thus makes him capable of accomplishing what he would otherwise be incapable of accomplishing.[71]
> —Mencius quoted by Master Funakoshi Gichin

In the same vein, we enter the reality of a moment to draw its very fullness. We aim at all-encompassing perfection – the very best we are capable of, filling the moment with unsurpassed meaning.

When we see excellence around us in *Budō* valor, technical ability, or other areas of endeavor, we "try to master it without hesitation."[72] We take it as a cue to do even better. If we see an excellent kick, we ask ourselves how to kick like that. If someone practices three times a day and

---

[69] *Ibid.*, 81.

[70] *Ibid.*, 89.

[71] Mencius, quoted in Master Funakoshi, *Kyōhan* (cited in note 6) at 247.

[72] *See* Master Funakoshi Gichin, *Karate-Dō Nyūmon: The Master Introductory Text* 46 (John Teramoto trans., Kodansha 1994) ("*Nyūmon*").

we don't, maybe it's a message for us to exert ourselves more. Or, if we see someone who never seems to improve, perhaps the same is true for us.[73]

If others think of difficulties as "just a lot of trouble," *Budō* demands that we rise to the challenge. "The greater the challenge the more we [are called upon to] take it on."[74] Without experiencing hardship, our dispositions might never "become firm and solid."[75]

I used to be fond of watching James Bond movies. 007 was a Karate man par excellence. Strangely, I'd never seen him in a *dōjō*, practicing his martial skills – he just "knew" Karate. Our approach to Karate-dō is different. We polish our skills day and night. Ohshima-sensei drives the message home, saying:

> You must face many opponents and many attacks. … You must practice your favorite technique 100,000 times before you can use it in any situation, against any opponent. Think of this: if your opponent has made 100,000 *oi-zuki* thinking of a realistic situation every time, do you think you can escape if you haven't practiced at least that many times?

It's not competition; it's a state of mind of always striving to be the best. There is a difference. If anything, we compete against ourselves, never against others. We surpass ourselves, always bearing in mind our faults. It has been said that "to be aware of [our] faults from moment to moment and work at this [for our whole lives] is what is called the 'Way.'"[76]

Faults or no faults, we train morning, noon and night – the energies around us change with each passing hour and season. Practicing only in the evening won't do. We must learn to perform Kata at all hours, always communing with the ever-changing energies around us.

Then, we can rise to any challenge. Then, knowing that no one is equal to us, we allow our martial courage to manifest itself with more ease.[77]

---

[73] *See ibid.*

[74] *See* Yamamoto (cited in note 24) at 89.

[75] *See ibid.*, 75.

[76] *See ibid.*, 69.

[77] *See ibid.*

CHAPTER 4
The Why of *Ki*

Yin and Yang have no beginning, action and stillness are not apparent, unless one knows the Way, who can hope to gain victory?[78]
—Ancient expression quoted by Master Funakoshi Gichin

Everything in the Universe is a manifestation of *Ki* – the energy that lies behind all creation. We may want to think of *Ki* as mental energy or mental awareness. Or, we may want to think of it as our internal GPS system that allows us to readjust and reposition ourselves in the environment as we move through it.

Ki is endowed with intelligence. It remembers. We can talk to and communicate with it. Encode it with the meanings of techniques and it will automatically find applications in real-life situations. Our conscious mind – slow and prone to making mistakes – is no match for it. Our challenge is to teach the *Ki* that we command by practicing tirelessly every single day with full intention and awareness. Then it will guide and protect us.

Once released, it keeps working as directed by us. It carries out our intentions. Sometimes its effects are immediate; sometimes we detect them after days, months, or even years. Sometimes the intended effects are thwarted by others, sometime we abort them ourselves either by abandoning our original intent or by sending conflicting *Ki* messages.

The Yin and Yang of *Ki*

Ki has the dual nature of Yin and Yang: the positive and negative aspects if you will. The Sun for example will assume Yang modality in relation to the Earth. Big is Yang, small is Yin. Light is Yang, shade is Yin. Fear is

---

[78] Master Funakoshi, *Karate Jutsu* (cited in note 15) at 37.

Yin, courage is Yang. Soft is Yin, hard is Yang. Receiving is Yin, giving is Yang. Young is Yang, old is Yin.[79]

These two aspects of *Ki* are relative depending on the surroundings and often oscillate between each other. Thus, to a ton of courage, a little courage will be Yin; to little softness, great softness will also be Yin. A big dog may be Yang while facing a puppy, but will assume a Yin aspect when matched with an even bigger dog.

We too are nothing but clusters of *Ki* placed in the midst of the *Ki* that surrounds us. The *Ki* within us may flow freely in constant exchange with the *Ki* around us – then we feel happy and full of vigor; or, it may stagnate in parts of our minds and bodies – then we may feel weak, and be prone to sickness and accidents.

Yin and Yang in Karate

> *The application principles of Karate are truly kaleidoscopic; however, in the case of fighting actually only two points really count: "sei" & "ki." The three ways to support the practical application of these points are (a) Observation (Go no sen), (b) Imperceptibility (Sen no sen), and (c) Transcendence (Sen).*[80]
>
> —Kyan Chōtoku-sensei

The ABC of Hands: Fullness & Emptiness

Because opponents we face in Karate are also creatures of *Ki*, we can analyze Karate practice as an interplay of *Ki* energies. Indeed, mastering *Ki* allows us not only to read and sense our opponents' intentions but also to enhance our ability to repel potential attacks and deliver more effective techniques.

The Yin and Yang of movement and stillness, activity and rest, and exhaling and inhaling has direct applications in Karate. Master Funakoshi

---

[79] On occasion some people attach opposite meanings to "Yin" and "Yang." That's OK. It's only a convention. The important thing is to be consistent in using these terms once they are defined one way or another.

[80] Kyan Chōtoku-sensei, quoted in Motobu-sensei, *Watashi no Karate-jutsu* (cited in note 17) at 47.

talked about "live" and "dead" hands. A striking hand is "live," carrying a payload of Yang energy while the other hand is "dead," waiting to be replenished with *Ki*. Upon completion of a strike, the lay of *Ki* land changes: The "live" hand becomes a "dead" hand, having just sent *Ki* away, while the "dead" hand returns from its lifeless Yin condition back to a "live" form.

Master Funakoshi viewed the Yin-and-Yang relation between two hands as the cardinal principle of Karate.[81] Without probing into the Yin-and-Yang nature of (a) the hand that just blocked[82] – referred to as *shini-te* (dead hand) (死に手) or *mete* (female hand) (雌手), and (b) the hand ready for action – referred to as *iki-te* (live hand) (活き手) or *ote* (male hand) (雄手), "how can victory be achieved?"[83] – he mused.

And so it is. There comes a moment in time when everything appears suspended and victory can be gained. Sometimes it is in the infinitesimal interval when Yin and Yang reverse their roles. If we (as Master Azato used to[84]) refer to our hands as *ki-sei* (奇正), with one hand thought of as strange or abnormal, or *ki* (奇), and the other as normal or correct, or *sei* (正), then the moment of change between *ki* and *sei* is where nothing seems to exist. Mastering the ability to change flawlessly from the one state to the other is what Karate is about.

Marrying the Hands

> *The blocking hand must be able to become the attacking hand in an instant. Blocking with one hand and then countering with the other is not true bujutsu. Real bujutsu presses forward and blocks and counters in the same motion.*[85]

> —Motobu Choki-sensei

---

[81] *See* Master Funakoshi, *Karate Jutsu* (cited in note 15) at 175.

[82] As we will see based on discussion of blocking techniques the hand that just blocked will generally (mostly in *Ki*-projecting blocks) become a *shini-te* hand, but not always.

[83] *See* Master Funakoshi, *Karate Jutsu* (cited in note 15) at 175.

[84] *See* Master Funakoshi, *Essence* (cited in note 1) at 75.

[85] Nakata Mizuhiko, *overseen by* Murakawa Kenji, *Collection of Sayings by Motobu Choki* (Joe Swift trans. 1978) ("*Collection of Sayings*"), quoted in Motobu-sensei, *Watashi no Karate-jutsu* (cited in note 17) at 31.

By incorporating the concepts of *iki-te/shini-te* or *ki-sei* into the study of Karate, techniques enter a new dimension of existence. The leading hand – ready to be deployed to block or disarm an incoming attack – will normally assume a *shini-te* condition, while, in the meantime, the other hand – in an energized *iki-te* form – will be ready for an instantaneous strike. Having assimilated these basics, we then learn to change the *ki-sei* nature of hands at will – to enable us to attack with *shini-te* by abruptly imparting it with energetic attributes of *iki-te* – a concept referred to by Master Funakoshi as *hen-shu*, or "switching of the hands."[86]

"As unpredictable as the vicissitudes of Heaven and the sudden shaking of the Earth," Funakoshi-sensei poetically reflected, *"hen-shu* can at times prove more effective than using the 'proper' hand."[87] Indeed, the ability to freely switch *Ki* attributes of hands in response to changing circumstances can reveal the parties' level of skill and decide the outcome of an encounter in a way "different than originally expected."[88]

The integration of *ki-sei* theory of hands into a functional application of power in combat situations is a notable contribution to Karate by Motobu Choki-sensei. It is expressed in the concept of *meoto-de* (夫婦手)[89] which does away with the rigid separation of hands as either defensive or offensive, which according to Motobu-sensei results in artificial inefficiencies in real combat. "[T]he lead hand," he explained, "can be used for both protecting and attacking concurrently." Only if and when the lead hand has failed its mission, "[t]he rear hand is used as a reserve."[90] In his famous *kamae*, Motobu Choki-sensei actually connects both hands, symbolically "marrying" them together.

Yin and Yang in Daily Life

Me-oto-di is an important principle of Karate that cannot be neglected. Those who study Kenpo should keep this principle in their

---

[86] *See* Master Funakoshi, *Karate Jutsu* (cited in note 15) at 36.

[87] *Ibid.*

[88] *Ibid.*

[89] Which can be translated as "hands of a married couple"; *meoto* being an alternate pronunciation of *fūfu* (夫婦), meaning married couple, and *de* (手) standing for hands.

[90] *See* Motobu-sensei, *Watashi no Karate-jutsu* (cited in note 17) at 83.

> *daily lives – such as when pouring sake, holding a bowl or chopsticks, etc. – and strive to master it through their own training.*[91]
>
> —Motobu Choki-sensei

True enough, when picking up food, our hand is in a receiving mode. It is a female, or Yin hand. We don't push the food away. Then, as it moves to our mouth, it changes into a giving hand, becoming a male, or Yang hand. As we open our mouth, expecting to receive – our mouth turns to a Yin receptacle. This too is an application of one of the principles of Karate, the principle of *ki-sei* hands.

For all its beauty and harmony, the *ki-sei* principle seems to elude many of us. How often do we meet Yin with Yin and Yang with Yang – in Karate and our daily lives? As a result, we create frictions, adding stress to our lives, sometimes ending up sick. Worse, the inability to harmonize with our partners in a *dōjō* often leads to unnecessary injuries and an unhealthy atmosphere. But practicing like this, we won't get an inkling of what *Budō* is about.

We practice the way of harmony in whatever we do. When someone expresses their opinion, we don't reject or contradict it. Whether we agree is beside the point. We acknowledge and respect it. Opportunities to practice abound in and out of a *dōjō*.

It may be OK for non-Karate people to live lives of separation without fully embracing the fields of energy within and around them. It may be OK for them to treat their own bodies as strangers. It may be OK for them to look at others as "them," rejecting, competing, trying to get ahead. To me those people are "half people," never realizing that there is only "us." But as followers of *Budō*, we know better. We accept and embrace, shedding delusions of separation. We know that the other person, in whatever relationship we may be, is just the other side of us. We connect, always seeking wholeness and harmony.

---

[91] *Ibid.*, 30. *"Me-oto-di,"* or 夫婦手 in kanji, translates as "wife-and-husband hands."

Protecting the Yin Side

> *I never thought about winning; I merely made up my mind never to let an opportunity slip by.*[92]
>
> —Uesugi Kenshin

The Four Enemies of *Budō* – Beware of *Kyo*

> *In order to react properly, you must free your mind by putting yourself in a state of tranquility.*[93]
>
> —Sugiyama Shojiro-sensei

Showing unbalanced Yin aspects in our posture or mental attitude may inadvertently invite an attack, exposing us to danger. The four major spiritual enemies of *Budō* – fear or *kyō* (恐), doubt or *gi* (疑), surprise or *kyō* (驚), and indecision or *waku* (惑) – referred to as the "four sicknesses of *Budō*" by Sugiyama-sensei[94] – place us in vulnerable states of extreme Yin against opponents whose unbridled Yang energies stand ready to pounce on perceived openings, taking advantage of our lapses in composure. At those times, we are in a hollow state of mind, susceptible to being attacked – a condition referred to as *kyo* (虚).

One aim of Karate training is to learn to suppress those Yin conditions. Projecting and circulating an undisturbed flow of *Ki* allows us to harmonize with the people around us. Our confidence grows. Showing tranquility of heart and maintaining our center in lower *tanden*, we keep the states of *kyo* at bay.

Kyo in Breathing

Breathing carries a dual Yin-and-Yang aspect: inhaling is Yin, exhaling is Yang. While inhaling we become more susceptible to an attack – entering into a *kyo* (虚) condition. The point of maximum vulnerability takes

---

[92] Uesugi Kenshin, quoted in Yamamoto (cited in note 24) at 87.

[93] Sugiyama-sensei, *11 Innovations* (cited in note 2) at 166.

[94] *Ibid.*, 15.

place just as inhaling phases out into exhaling. At this point Yin and Yang reverse their cycle.

This momentary inaction in breathing resembles the momentary stillness of a pendulum at its maximum displacement point. This momentary settlement of *Ki* is referred to as *itsuki* (居着き). People who shoot at coins thrown in the air often take advantage of it, shooting when the coin's upward rise culminates at the highest point in a hollow condition of stillness.

As breathe we must, we need to take good care to protect ourselves when breathing in. Ideally, we need to project some Yang energies even when inhaling. For instance, while breathing in, we may want to project *Ki* to negate its Yin aspect. We try to make inhales short and exhales long, never showing our breathing to the opponent, and always trying to execute techniques, including blocks, on an exhale.

Kyo on Commitment

Between committing to use a technique and actually executing it, there is an interval, however short. Intention, conscious or not, initiates every action we take. You may have noticed that sometimes as soon as we commit to take an action, say park a car in an empty space, someone appears there before us, even though the space was empty for a long time before we came into the picture.

What happens is that our intention allocated to the empty parking space creates a *Ki* opening – Yin by nature – which invites Yang energies to fill in the space in form of a car. Just before someone preempted us, we may have become distracted, losing our *tanden* connection. Or, our intention was too weak to begin with. Be that as it may, someone managed to exploit the moment of our vulnerability.

Similarly in Karate, in the interval between our commitment to perform a technique and its execution, we momentarily enter into a *kyo* (虚) condition, becoming vulnerable to a preemptive block or attack. Conversely, we may more easily block and thwart an attack when our partner has just made a commitment to attack. We call such preemptive action *sen-no-sen*, or *sen-sen-no-sen*.

Kyo on Execution

If our commitment to take action is not interrupted, latent Yang energies move in physically realizing our intention by executing the technique. Once the action is complete, Yang energies of the striking limb are exhausted and another momentary state of *kyo* may appear if we do not quickly reestablish the Yin-and-Yang balance. At such a time, we become vulnerable to a counterattack.

To guard against such imbalance, we stress the importance of *hiki-te* during training. The moment we complete an action with one hand, the other hand – *hiki-te* – becomes fully Yang-energized, ready for another action.[95] In fact, in order to avoid a momentary deficit of Yang energies, we are often told to initiate our *hiki-te* motion slightly before activating the other hand.

This brings to mind another episode from my honeymoon. One day, looking for parking on a busy street, to my delight I spotted an empty space for my somewhat over-sized car (it was my wedding after all!). After a bit of struggle I managed to squeeze the big car neatly in place. As luck would have it, the spot was reserved for business vehicles. Little did I know that there was a cop patiently watching my efforts, just waiting until I completed the maneuver. I left the car feeling good about myself and my luck, throwing the concept of *zanshin* (of which I say more later) to the wind in my momentary elation. No sooner had I done so than the cop dropped a ticket on the windshield. You could say that he engaged in *go-no-sen* tactics – attacking after I had taken the initiative. Or perhaps it was an example of a deftly executed *mikiri* on his part. Hard to say.

In Karate too I observe people who, having just completed a technique, lower their guard, opening themselves to an immediate counterattack. Master Funakoshi, for whom there were no second chances in Karate, would not be pleased. If striking, our first technique must be our last. Otherwise, our moment of vulnerability following a failed attack could be exploited by a strong and now more enraged opponent.

---

[95] I will explore the "why" of *hiki-te* in more detail in a separate section devoted to this subject.

Kyo on Indecision

> *Whenever you are ordered to do anything at all, you should agree on the spot. For a <u>bushi</u>, to reflect this way and that before one does something is the root of cowardice.*[96]
>
> —Yamamoto Tsunetomo

Years ago, a friend who is a good and careful driver bought her first hybrid car, enjoying it tremendously. On occasions however she was stumped when trying to move from a side road into unrelenting traffic. Cars wouldn't slow down to let her in. She was completely nonplussed.

I suggested that she first strongly project her *Ki* into her intended maneuver so that other drivers take notice. Otherwise, they would keep driving, oblivious of her presence, taking advantage of a clear pathway in front of them.

In Karate too, we must project *Ki* toward our partners. We do so to enter their energy body. Sending soft energies of love and peace will help us accomplish this. Trying to exert pressure on the opponent by sending strong Yang-*Ki* towards them will make it more difficult – the opponents will instinctively resist such *Ki*, pushing it away.

As we blend in with the *Ki* of our opponents, we continuously receive their *Ki*. This is not difficult – we simultaneously send and receive *Ki* all the time. If we don't mix our mutual *Ki* we may not be able to read our partners' intentions quickly enough. If we don't project *Ki*, some mean-spirited people may take it as a weakness and look at us as convenient punching bags for venting their aggression.

But if we decide to act, we must act, forgetting everything else as if our lives depended on it. If we vacillate, we send a clear signal to our partners of our momentary vulnerability.

Kyo on Distraction

> *One could spit in the opponent's face, emit a kiai, stamp one's foot or clap one's hands to distract the opponent as other means of defensive*

---

[96] Yamamoto (cited in note 24) at 232.

actions. Therefore, keeping in mind these methods, one will be able to easily control an opponent with a weapon."[97]

—Master Funakoshi Gichin

Again and again when sparring with beginners, I notice that in the process they think of some unrelated things (who knows what), sometimes looking at what others are doing, or listening to what others are saying. I want to throw up my hands in despair.

Karate practice, for all its serious *Budō* implications, is a time to fully concentrate on what we do. Once distracted, the *Ki* of our energy mind and body becomes momentarily disrupted, and the opponent can quickly take advantage of it.

From a childish example of suddenly pointing something up above, to more typical *kumite* faints of pretending to attack one area of the body in order to attack another, or kicking a leg to divert attention, or suddenly pressing a leading hand while executing a punch, the principle and the method are the same: throw the opponent into a momentary *kyo* condition where their flow of *Ki* is momentarily put out of whack; either halted or forced to change direction.

To achieve an undisturbed concentration, we must free our minds and, as Sugiyama-sensei taught, "strive for a mental state of 'nothingness.'"[98] Regardless whether we are touched, punched, kicked, or shouted at we must maintain undisturbed composure. As Sugiyama-sensei explained:

> The word *"Karate"* implies lack of ego and achieving a state where outside influences cannot interrupt or disturb your concentration. ... The word *Karate* is derived from the "nothingness" (*mu*) of *zen* Buddhism. This "nothingness" gives us freedom from the psychological obstruction posed by fear. ... Therefore, *mu* is the very essence of *Karate*.[99]

---

[97] Master Funakoshi, *Kyōhan* (cited in note 6) at 233.
[98] Sugiyama-sensei, *11 Innovations* (cited in note 2) at 10.
[99] *Ibid.*

Our ability to maintain composure and concentration on a *dōjō* floor has awesome implications for our entire lives. If we cannot concentrate in a *dōjō*, the chances are we cannot concentrate when our business, livelihood or personal relationships are at stake. The ability of single-minded concentration in Karate may be the most important lesson to carry to other areas of our lives to attain our goals and fulfill our dreams.

Kyo on Attachment

Years ago, I asked a fellow practitioner who had just lost his last match in a *kumite* tournament whether he had wanted to win. He looked at me in disbelief. "Naturally I wanted to win," he answered.

Inflexibly holding on to personal desires can create openings in our minds that others can exploit. Attachments to thoughts blur our spiritual vision. With our minds restlessly chasing our transient desires, we don't see things clearly. Let's polish the mirrors of our minds and quiet our souls by eliminating those attachments. Let's aim at a spiritual state of *meikyō shisui*[100] by becoming clear shining mirrors reflecting the still, undisturbed waters of *Ki* around us. Then our minds will be tranquil and serene. We will see things as they truly are.

Kyo in Posture

Good instructors insist on proper posture. They say that *Shōtō-kan's* techniques are large, expansive, with practitioners' chests confidently open. Indeed, practicing like this instills confidence as the posture of form changes the quality of *Ki* flowing in and out of our bodies.

On the other hand, observing small, furtive-looking techniques in others I sense lack of confidence emanating from those forms which could be interpreted as fear by the opponents. The flow of energy tends to be shallow, its passage often blocked along the way by incorrect posture, affecting our mind, spirit, and emotions. Paradoxically, improper training of Karate – without minute attention to optimal form – can increase

---

[100] In kanji, 明鏡止水 – a clear and undisturbed mind, as a polished mirror and still water.

the chances of finding ourselves in danger by creating inadvertent *kyo* conditions in our posture. That's the last thing we want.

Ki Is Knowledge

> *He who is able to read circumstances in his mind before they tran-*
> *spire, to see the playing out of opposing forces yet to begin, as if with*
> *eyes behind one's head, is capable of knowing the path to certain*
> *victory.*[101]
>
> —Master Funakoshi Gichin

In the *Maxims for the Trainee* part of *Karate-Dō Kyōhan*, Master Funakoshi distilled for us the wisdom of the ancients:

> Know the enemy and know yourself; in a hundred battles you
> will never be in peril. When you are ignorant of the enemy but
> know yourself, your chances of winning or losing are equal. If
> you are ignorant of the enemy and yourself, you are certain in
> every battle to be in peril.[102]

That's unarguable wisdom. Yet, my mind is restless. I need more. What does it mean? How do we know ourselves? How do we know our enemy? How do we really know?

Typical explanations equate knowledge of an opponent with knowing their favorite techniques, size, or other external attributes. Yes, it may be helpful to know that a person has a strong punch or powerful kick. Yet, in the heat of battle there is little time to engage in mental analysis of what the other person is capable of doing. We must free our minds from needless clutter and be ready for anything that may come.

As I understand it, the secret lies in knowing our opponent's *Ki*. As mentioned before, *Ki* is endowed with intelligence. The *Ki* we emit displays information about us. *Ki* never lies. I suspect – but more research would be welcome – that *Ki* conveys all our secrets and history – in fact

---

[101] Master Funakoshi, *Essence* (cited in note 1) at 68.
[102] Master Funakoshi, *Kyōhan* (cited in note 6) at 248.

everything about us. To determine whether a person's *Ki* is strong or weak, healthy or sick is relatively easy. But what if we could penetrate deeper into our opponent's *Ki*? Perhaps we could know everything.

Sugiyama-sensei devoted his later years to creating a *Ki*-radar methodology for detecting our opponent's intent to execute Karate techniques. Perhaps we could go further and implant our *Ki* within their *Ki*, making it temporarily our own. The ability to fuse our individual *Ki* could allow us to effortlessly reach the *Budō* ideal of ending fighting – not by winning a hundred battles in one hundred encounters, but by subduing the enemy without a fight.[103]

To read an opponent's *Ki* we must tap into it, making it part of our own *Ki* circulation. While most *Ki* information flows through our *chakras*, we absorb it with our entire bodies. Thus, we gather information through our middle *tanden*, or *chū-tanden* in Japanese, the gushing springs of our feet (*yong-quan*, or *yū-sen* in Japanese) and our palm geysers (*lao-gong*, or *rō-kyu* in Japanese), and our crown *chakra* (*bai-hui*, or *hyaku-e* in Japanese).

We absorb the *Ki* of our opponent through our third-eye *chakra* located between our eyebrows, referred to in Japanese as upper *tanden*, or *jō-tanden*. Indeed, in Karate we do not look at our opponent directly – that would make us vulnerable, slowing our reactions, making us miss things. We look through our peripheral vision centered on our third-eye *chakra*. Nevertheless, as demonstrated by the venerable Sugiyama-sensei, even our peripheral vision may not register a strike delivered with lightning speed. That's why we must train our ability to detect our opponent's moves at their mental inception.[104] If we can't, no matter how strong our punches are, we will lose.

This ability to read the opponent's *Ki*, however, is not enough. They may still overpower us with their energy, rendering us defenseless. It is even more important to implant within them *Ki* that we command, *Ki*

---

[103] *See ibid.*

[104] *See* Sugiyama-sensei, *11 Innovations* (cited in note 2) at 165 – 66, discussing experiments measuring reaction time of an experienced *Karate-ka's* punch upon seeing a flash of light; in those experiments, it took 170 milliseconds to recognize that the light was on, 30 milliseconds to start a punch and 50 milliseconds to finish it, for the total of 250 milliseconds from the time the light went on (or, to translate to Karate practice, from the time when the partner's physical motion began).

that carries information that we encode. However you measure it, in the end, every encounter turns into a contest of *Ki*.

A *Ki* Master Class: Without Fear or Hostility

What happens on the physical plane seems but an extension of what is being played out in the world of *Ki* where all battles are decided. Therefore well-nourished martial *Ki* is Karate's primary weapon. We cultivate it, polish it, and broaden its bandwidth every day. No outward technique, threat or weapon can rival it. Making the *Ki* flowing from our minds and hearts strong, all-encompassing, and pure of temporary attachments is what *Budō* training is all about.

A Contest of *Ki* – The Story of Bushi Matsumura and Karate Uehara

As the story goes, the legendary Bushi Matsumura Sōkon, still in his late 20s, defeated in a match the famous "Karate" Uehara[105] – until then an invincible martial artist – without throwing a single blow.[106] One day, Bushi Matsumura, of a noble Okinawan pedigree, stood dejected in Uehara's metal shop, having just been dismissed as a Karate instructor to the lord of the castle, now only to be challenged to a match by a mere shopkeeper. Uehara, still in his prime, around 43 years of age, doubtless thought little of this youngster, regardless of his social standing and royal connections because, in his view, "in martial arts there's no difference between rich and poor, high and low."[107]

The next morning, confident in his martial skills, he was closing distance on Bushi Matsumura who stood motionless in a nonchalant-like posture, chin resting on his shoulder yet eyes emitting a strangely fierce glare. With each attempt to attack, however, an invisible power arrested Uehara's movements. Even his powerful *kiai* had no visible effect on his opponent. Again and again he tried, only to meet with the same result.

---

[105] I assume his name was "Tō-de (Chinese-hands) Uehara" since, as I understand it, the term "Karate" was not yet used in Okinawa at the time of this legendary encounter.

[106] The story as recounted by Master Funakoshi in *Nyūmon* (cited in note 70) at 101 – 08; *see also* Master Funakoshi, *My Way of Life* (cited in note 14) at 21 – 29.

[107] *Ibid.*, 104.

He broke into a copious sweat; a sense of fear he had never known overwhelmed him.

Unaccustomed to losing, Uehara came "flying at Bushi Matsumura with the energy of a fireball and the will to smash through a massive rock." But then, just before making contact, Bushi Matsumura let off an "almost inhuman, reverberating like thunder" shout that paralyzed Uehara who dropped to his knees in defeat.[108]

"I couldn't move my hands or feet," confessed Uehara upon surrender. "I was terrified of your eyes, terrified of your face, of your voice. I could feel no hostility, no fighting spirit – all I felt was fear."[109]

If Uehara's technical skills were superior, the unmatched power of Bushi Matsumura's *Ki* showed little respect for them. Indeed, removed from the realm of *Ki*, the story may sound like a Karate fairytale. Add *Ki* dimension, and the story suddenly comes down to Earth, evoking similar incidents from our own lives.

The main if not the only reason for our practice is to cultivate and steel strong *Ki* to the point that physical fighting is no longer necessary. May the story of the Uehara-Matsumura duel lead us along this path.

Again and again, within minutes of my being next to an ostensibly hostile person, their attitude markedly changes. Sometimes, being around an obnoxious individual, I check my initial impulse to react, just waiting, doing nothing. Soon that person's disposition mellows, turning into kindness. Apparently, the blending of mutual *Ki* can have a strangely pacifying effect.

I don't think we can transform our adversaries' fighting intention by showing fear or hostility toward them. Although both are perfectly natural defensive reactions they reflect our attachments to life, which make us vulnerable, preventing us from seeing things as they truly are. Once fear overwhelms us, we are powerless to transform our opponents' *Ki*. Fear is a sign of capitulation: the *Ki* at our command recedes, telling them that we are at their mercy. Hostility toward opponents likewise prevents us from changing their *Ki*. It merely eggs them on to a contest and show of force.

---

[108] *Ibid.*, 107 – 08.

[109] *Ibid.*, 108.

To progress in Karate we must learn to control hostile and fearful reactions. If we want to change opponents' aggressive intentions we must drown them with fearless *Ki* devoid of any sign of enmity toward them.

One Samurai's *Ki* Conquers Armies

One person's *Ki* can overpower the *Ki* of several opponents, as discussed in ancient Karate annals. In the case of Watanabe Satoru, a famous samurai of feudal Japan, his indomitable *Ki* deterred armies of men.

Tōdō Takatora, a lord in the Tokugawa shogunate, awarded Watanabe an unheard-of stipend of 20,000 *koku* (a samurai's income was measured in units of rice volume called *koku*).[110] Hearing this, another lord laughed at such an obvious extravagance, "However strong Watanabe Satoru may be, he could always be overpowered by a gang of men."[111] "Not so," replied Takatora:

> If I were to gather a hundred, even two hundred obscure sa-
> murai about me, my enemies could still crush them. But if they
> hear that I am protected by the famous Watanabe Satoru, most
> of my enemies will be too frightened to attack.[112]

True enough, Watanabe's mere presence lent an air of invincibility to Takatora's ranks, assuring many subsequent victories. The perception of his power made opposing armies think twice before attacking. Tales of his prowess and valor cloaked the group with an invisible suit of *Ki* armor, sowing fear among and deterring external enemies.

The Why of Karate Teaching

Indeed. If Karate is not meant for fighting, why even bother, some might say. We can learn techniques and the meaning of Kata movements from books, videos or friends. Why get fitted up in a fancy *gi* and pay monthly

---

[110] Matsushita Konosuke (founder of Panasonic), *Velvet Glove, Iron Fist: And 101 Other Dimensions of Leadership* 16 – 17 (PHP Institute 1991).

[111] *Ibid.*

[112] *Ibid.*, 17.

dues if all this stuff is freely available on YouTube? Just to get a sparring partner?

But the map of Karate's forms and techniques is not its territory. *Ki* is the answer. Often, without even realizing it, by signing up with Karate teachers we are in fact asking (and allowing) them to expand, improve and empower the *Ki* that is at our disposal. Yes, they will teach us through Karate forms, but the essence is not in the techniques. The essence lies in assimilating their *Ki*. On a daily basis, we go to the *dōjō* and commune with our teachers' *Ki*, hanging out on every word they say, emulating the slightest movements of their bodies – we want to be just like them. In the process, the teachers' *Ki* grows on us, becoming our own. As suggested earlier, their *Ki* contains all their knowledge. Once we assimilate it, we have that knowledge too. We can uncover its contents, mysteries and secrets on our own.

At least this is my idea of a *sensei* – a term traditionally reserved to very few professions. The concept carries grave responsibility for students and teachers alike. Choosing a teacher can magically transform our lives – to great benefit or utter ruin. Teachers' technical skills, fame or lineage traced to other teachers should be the least of our concern. More than anything else, their moral and martial attitudes must be of the highest grade. They – even more than students – must work on improving themselves at all times.

Some *dōjō* have deviated from the traditional concept. There, they "sell" teaching Karate forms, giving instructions on how to fight. Once training (*renshū*) is over, those teachers' jobs are finished. What kind of Karate can we learn there?

Cultivating Strong and Healthy *Ki*

> To speak of the things that are important for a samurai ... the most fundamental thing is first to commit one's life unstintingly to one's lord. ... [O]ne should fully develop oneself in the virtues of wisdom (<u>chi</u>), fellow feeling (<u>jin</u>) and courage (<u>yū</u>). ... "[I]t is when one is calm and composed that one's strength in all these skills will come forth."[113]
>
> —Yamamoto Tsunetomo

---

[113] Yamamoto (cited in note 24) at 76 – 77.

Opening *Ki* Channels

The mind – through its will power – activates and moves *Ki*, whether consciously or not. The mind directs; *Ki* delivers the mind's message. If we intend to move our body, upon our mind's command, *Ki* propels it into motion.

To increase effectiveness of our techniques we must therefore foster strong but flexible will power and free and easy flow of *Ki* through our body's bones, sinews and joints.

Our will power will increase if we lead lives of integrity and courage, without petty attachments to things, thoughts or ideas. Our bodies will show corresponding strength, vitality and resilience. Let's not forget, our bodies and minds constitute one integral whole, each reflecting the other. Training one means training the other.

Tension and Relaxation

Lethargic, stressed-out and vigorless bodies resist *Ki* movement. To allow *Ki* to travel through our bodies freely and with dexterity, we must eliminate our inhibitions and temporal attachments from our minds and bodies by learning how to totally relax. Without the ability to fully relax, the free flow of *Ki* may be arrested or retarded, creating energy imbalance, pain or sickness. To relax, we must also know how to tense our bodies and be able to distinguish between the two conditions.

This is easier said than done. In my experience, some beginners have no idea how to relax. Granted, teachers exhort them repeatedly not to use any power, just relax. But if they don't know how to, just saying "relax" is of little help. Indeed, it may confuse them even more, exacerbating the problem. The general silence on the subjects of *Ki* and Yin and Yang in an average *dōjō* certainly does not help.

Let's start by regularly and thoroughly stretching our bodies with proper breathing and awareness, mindfully moving *Ki* all over them. We must know and feel the difference between light and heavy conditions, and achieve the ability to nimbly switch between them. *Maki-wara* and Kata practice are invaluable tools. When breaking a hold of a partner, let's think which hand is light (or lighter) and which heavy (or heavier). Why does it matter? Does striking using ordinary physical strength or pure *Ki* movement feel more effective? Do we maintain balance when we move? How does correct posture affect the *Ki* we deploy while striking? Can we tell the difference?

Hopefully, through Karate practice and continuous cultivation of *Ki*, we will reach a state where our minds and bodies will become impenetrable to any enemy. Then we will be walking examples of bodies "hard within and dense without" that "can never be penetrated."[114]

Zazen

> *Breath is the gateway between the physical and mental, and, if a learner sits down to meditate in the morning he should also oscillate the limbs when finished in order to restore energy.*[115]
>
> —Motobu Choki-sensei

For a long time, I have been combining my Karate practice with sitting *zazen*, breathing slowly, centering my entire being in *tanden*, absorbing and re-circulating the *Ki* of the Universe. I often feel that for the development of strong *Ki* and *tanden* concentration, sitting *zazen* even for twenty minutes is equivalent to an hour spent on formal Karate training. More important, regular *zazen* practice clears my mind of delusions that inhibit my progress in martial arts.

Reportedly, ancient samurai had a saying *"zazen* seven, *ken* three" (where *"ken"* refers to a sword, like in Kendo), which reminded them to put the spiritual side of training before the physical. Although I cannot vouch for the authenticity of this adage, I find the message fully applicable to Karate and illustrative of its overall philosophy.

We may sit *zazen*, grounding our bodies in a well-balanced traditional *kekka-fuza* (full lotus) or *hanka-fuza* (half lotus) posture on a *zafu* cushion as practiced in Buddhist temples. We may also sit in *seiza* – a sitting position familiar from our *dōjō* – with equal effect. We join our hands in

---

[114] Master Funakoshi, *Kyōhan* (cited in note 6) at 248.

[115] Quoted in Motobu-sensei, *Watashi no Karate-jutsu* (cited in note 17) at 82.

the traditional *hokkai-jō-in*[116] meditation *mudra*, placing the fingers of our left hand over the fingers of our right hand, palms up, gently touching the tips of our thumbs together. Placing the tip of our tongue against the roof of our mouth and keeping our mouth closed, we gaze downward at about 45-degree angle toward a blank wall in front of us. We sit and we breathe – in unison with the Universe.

More challenging is to maintain focus in *tanden* not only when we sit but also while moving. Yes, we can walk in the mental state of *zazen* – an exercise referred to as "walking zen," or *kinhin* – as practiced in some Buddhist temples, moving slowly clockwise in a circle at the conclusion of formal sitting zen meditation.[117] Ideally, we want to transfer the *zazen* state of mind to our Karate.

The Yin and Yang of Posture

A good posture reflects good *Ki* circulation and denotes the level of our martial arts skill. I am convinced that bad posture places artificial kinks along our energy channels, resulting in an imbalance of *Ki* and a variety of ailments and injuries.

We are small Yin creatures in relation to the giant Earth. In our Karate practice we often hold on tight to our Mother Earth. We grip it with our feet, sinking our energies downward, and give our techniques additional boosts of earthly energy by stomping the ground with *fumi-komi*. (As we do so, the energy we forcefully shoot onto the floor through our feet re-bounds toward our techniques.) As a result, we become creatures of the Earth, struggling, fighting, competing. Our shoulders rise up, our head sinks in. The nape of our neck curves in a pigeon-like fashion, obstructing the free flow of *Ki* through our spine.

In the fervor of practice we often forget a more potent power – the power of Heaven. In relation to the *Ki* above, the *Ki* of the Earth is Yin. It is like water to the fire of the Sun and the skies – the big Yang. To rebalance our energies and keep our meridian pathways unblocked, we need to strengthen our connection to the *Ki* from above. Our heads should have

---

[116] There are other hands positions used for meditation but this is the most common.

[117] Various forms of standing meditation are also common within Qigong.

a feeling of being suspended from the sky by a thread of heavenly *Ki*; our spines straightened; our bodies linking the energies up above with those down below. Our breathing should take good account of this principle.

We connect to both sources of energy: the Heaven and the Earth. We respect them both. Just raising our spirit high would be disastrous to our Karate practice. We must equally respect our Mother Earth, caring for it, treading ever so lightly upon it. Observing how cats walk might be a good way to start.

If we can maintain constant connection with heavenly *Ki*, our bodies will become lighter, our spirits sprightlier. We will move more nimbly, react faster. Our hips and knees, relieved of redundant weight, will reward us with a sense of alacrity. Our Karate will be more inspired and our techniques will flow more freely.

Kokyū-hō

> *A weak man breathes at the shoulders. An ordinary man breathes at his abdomen. A courageous man breathes at the tanden (lower abdomen). A true man breathes at the feet.*[118]
>
> —An old saying

We can improve our posture by proper breathing – a subject rarely studied, analyzed or explored in a typical *dōjō*. Yet, our breathing, which, while independent, can boost the movement of *Ki* inside and the release of *Ki* outside our bodies, affects the quality and strength of our techniques and *kime*. I would even suggest that the way we breathe determines how strong, healthy, happy, or prosperous we can become.

We breathe through our skin, our feet, our hands, our eyes and our chakras. With time, proper circulation of *Ki* will cleanse our bodies from stagnant *Ki* accumulations.

We might try *Ki* breathing exercises – *kokyū-hō* or *kikō* in Japanese. These exercises consist of patterns of circulating *Ki* throughout our bodies in tandem with different patterns of breathing. We might also adopt some Qigong *Ki* purification, enhancement and healing practices.

---

[118] Quoted in Ohshima-sensei, *Notes on Training* (cited in note 27) at 215.

For example, Nishino Kōzō-sensei's school in Tokyo offers *kokyū-hō* classes, which I followed for years at Sugiyama-sensei's suggestion. Nishino-sensei has developed an original method of breathing from the feet while moving *Ki* throughout the body. But it is not the only system. There are other schools. In fact, for years I have been obsessed with creating a method of my own more suitable for Karate. As breathing is intimately connected with *Ki* circulation throughout our bodies, some methods may be harmful to our health. For that reason, I would caution against trying to experiment with untested breathing methods on your own.

Not surprisingly, some people think of breathing methods in proprietary terms. Nishino-sensei tells a story of Anna Pavlova, a super-ballerina from Russia who in 1922 performed on stage in Japan. Asked about the secret of one of her superior poses, she said, "I draw in air from the tips of my toes, slowly bring it up, then send it from my shoulders to the tips of my fingers so that my entire body feels like it is floating, and I can continue to keep the pose as long as I like." A famous kabuki actor snuck up every night posing as a stage hand to discover her breathing secrets – "one genius trying to learn trade secrets from another."[119]

One *kokyū-hō* exercise I find particular beneficial is *karin*; also referred to as *suwaishō*. I first saw this exercise in a Karate *dōjō*, only to get my fill of it in Kozo Nishino-sensei's school, where students performed it ad nauseam. While performing *karin* – as Nishino-sensei calls it – I center myself in my *tanden* and, without using muscular strength and in a state of total relaxation, release *Ki* through my swinging arms, initiating each rotation from my hips – energy moving gently up, vertebra by vertebra. My posture is straight, my knees are relaxed, and my head feels like it is being suspended from above.

I use *kokyū-hō* not only to open up clogged up energy paths, purify my *Ki*, and sharpen my *Ki* awareness but also to help me better employ empty-and-full, and light-and-heavy conditions of my body. Breathing exercises enhance my ability to collect *Ki* in my bones and sinews. Indeed, breathing through the bones is crucial to the collection of *Ki* from around us and the effective application of strength and *kime* in our techniques.

---

[119] *See* Kozo Nishino, *The Breath of Life: Using the Power of Ki for Maximum Vitality* 57 – 58 (Kodansha 1997).

Inen Exercises

Focusing intention on any object or parts of our body, we energize them with *Ki*. We call such focused intention *inen* in Japanese. When we defocus, the energy quiets down.

To better understand the difference between light-and-heavy conditions, we could play with alternating *inen* in different parts of our bodies. For example, we could alternate light-and-heavy feeling in our forearms by placing them in front of us parallel to the floor, or by forming a fighting *kamae*. The heavy forearm will naturally tend to sink downward, while the light forearm will levitate upward like a feather effortlessly floating in the air.[120]

To better understand our *Ki* channels, we could experiment with energizing parts of our spines and observe the effect it has on the ulna of our forearms. We will notice that doing *inen* on our spines induces *Ki* generation in the ulna.[121] We could also experiment with clenching our individual fingers to detect corresponding effects on other parts of our bodies.

Inen exercises have a direct application in Karate, making our blocking and striking more effective and improving our *kumite* skills. Furthermore, they allow us to gradually identify ourselves and the world around us with *Ki* – making our movements float in the air, fully integrated with our surroundings, becoming elusive and inaccessible to attacks.

Chi-ishi

> *Most kinds of training equipment used in Karate have been handed throughout the tradition from long ago. Despite some groups describing this type of equipment as primitive and abandoning its use, I must emphasize the contrary; it is not archaic nor should it be ignored.*[122]
>
> —Motobu Choki-sensei

---

[120] More *inen* and similar exercises can be found in Sugiyama-sensei's books: *11 Innovation in Karate* (cited in note 2) and *Aura, Ki & Healing* (1999).

[121] *See* Sugiyama-sensei, *11 Innovations* (cited in note 2) at 242.

[122] Quoted in Motobu-sensei, *Watashi no Karate-jutsu* (cited in note17) at 87.

I have never seen *chi-ishi* – typically round weights of various sizes with straight handles of Okinawan origin – in any *Shōtō-kan dōjō*. Many *Shōtō-kan* practitioners have never even heard of them. Why is this? Because other schools use them? How small-minded, especially bearing in mind Master Funakoshi's view that, in essence, there are no Karate "styles" and all Karate is one.

Chi-ishi practice helps me improve and strengthen my *Ki* circulation. I see no reason why Karate schools other than *Gōjū-ryū* (where it is used mainly for building strength) should not adopt this useful practice tool.

I hope that with Karate entering the Olympic stage, a movement will rise to reconnect branches of various schools into a unified whole. Each style has its own strengths and insights. Drawing on the best of different traditions could lift Karate to yet-unimagined heights.

A Bunch of BS or the Key to Karate Mastery

Some people doubt or even deny the existence of *Ki*. It sounds to them like a lot of BS. Sugiyama-sensei had a way of dealing with such doubters by allowing them to see their own *Ki* and the *Ki* aura of others with their own eyes. Call it *Ki* or call it by any other name, its existence and attributes cannot be denied.

True, you can spend your whole life practicing Karate without incorporating the concept of *Ki*, just by using your muscular strength without even differentiating between the Yin and Yang of techniques. Indisputably, some people will master Karate instinctively without theorizing about it. Too much theory could even confuse them. Others, however, will repeat the physical motions of Karate forms and *waza*, never really progressing. As their physical prowess declines with age – a universal truth for all of us – so does their Karate. Hopefully, practicing Karate based on Yin-and-Yang principles of *Ki* can slow down our aging process while retaining our vitality.[123]

---

[123] See examples of longevity among distinguished martial artists given by Master Funakoshi in his *Karate Jutsu* (cited in note 15) at 29.

Putting It All Together

We initiate a punch by our mind's intention to do so. The intention creates a Yin vessel waiting to be filled in with Yang energy which we deliver in the form of a physical strike. Our intention may be conscious or involuntary. As soon as it is formed, our mind enters into a momentary Yin condition, creating a hollow state of *kyo*.

Because Yang powers are naturally attracted to Yin energy, they automatically move in to meet a Yin imprint created by our mind. If fact, we could deliver a strong punch even without deliberately forcing the flow of Yang *Ki* – a punch might still manifest itself of its own accord as long as we had enough Yang energies stored within us.

We must concentrate on delivering a laser-like, destructive *Ki* impulse to a point behind our opponent's body. Attempts to propel our punches by added physical force will not only slow them down and sabotage our focus but may prevent full deployment of the *Ki* at our disposal. I will explore ways to deliver the most effective punch in the next chapter *The Why of Kime*.

On the other hand, to protect against aggressive action, we must develop skills allowing us to detect – without thinking – the opponent's intention to attack. As soon as we sense such intention, before the opponent has initiated any physical action, we must act. We could (a) execute a pre-emptive attack at that time, (b) block and simultaneously counter-attack with the non-blocking hand, (c) block and instantaneously counter with the blocking hand, or (d) step away into a zone of safety ready for our countering technique. Doing nothing, waiting until the opponent's physical action begins is too late. The risk of getting hit at this point has multiplied.

CHAPTER 5

The Why of *Kime*

*The main objective in Karate is to finish your opponent with one blow. This means <u>focusing</u> all the power you have in one spot and momentarily supporting that spot with your entire body. This focus is called **kime**.*[124]

—Sugiyama Shojiro-sensei

Seeing is Believing

A two-foot wide, three-foot long and two-inch thick wooden board hung from the rafters of a restaurant that doubled as Motobu Choki-sensei's *dōjō*. Motobu-sensei asked a visiting *Karate-ka* if he could break it with his fist placed just about an inch away from the board. After saying a little prayer, the visitor struck it with all the power he had but the board merely bounced off with a thud. Next, Motobu-sensei's student who happened to be around took up the challenge – with no better results. "Watch closely," said Motobu-sensei, placing his fist about an inch away, and, sounding off a *kiai*, instantly shattered the board into two neat pieces that fell to the ground.[125]

Kime: The Heart of Karate

Genuine Karate is more than the outer beauty of its form. It's a world where by constantly receiving, collecting and projecting *Ki*, practitioners stay constantly aware of their surroundings. It's a world where soft energies of relaxation can spontaneously change into hardness to harmonize with ever-changing circumstances. A world where latent Yang *Ki* can instantly turn into the ultimate hardness of *kime* – the laser-like focused

---

[124] Sugiyama-sensei, *11 Innovations* (cited in note 2) at 13.

[125] As related in Nakata, *Collection of Sayings* (cited in note 85), quoted in Motobu-sensei, *Watashi no Karate-jutsu* (cited in note 17) at 33.

concentration of the entire body, spirit and mind at the moment of impact. This sudden spike of *Ki* power injected through a target of attack, followed by a continuous flow of *Ki* through sustained mental concentration (*zanshin*), is what makes *Budō* Karate so lethal.

Fully developed *kime* has three fundamental components which, converged, can produce an astounding force. They are streams of three *Ki* vectors from which focused power emanates: the *tanden* vector, the striking-arm vector, and the eye vector.[126]

The Why of *Maki-wara* Training

> I think I am in no way exaggerating when I say that practice with maki-wara *is the keystone in the creation of strong weapons. ... Incidentally, anyone who practices Karate as a form of calisthenics need not use a* maki-wara: *he may practice and go through all the necessary actions without ever striking a blow.*[127]
>
> —Master Funakoshi Gichin

I often wonder if mastering the ability to turn the *Ki* we harness with our minds and bodies into sudden explosive *kime* is possible without regular *maki-wara* practice. I am simply not aware of any better way to develop and refine strong *kime*.

Master Funakoshi did not know any practitioner of the art who did not regularly use *maki-wara*. Fast forward a century: I know hardly anyone who integrates substantial *maki-wara* practice into their daily Karate routine. In an ironic twist, in several *dōjō* I had been repeatedly admonished not to use it: too noisy and disturbing to other students, being a common justification.

I may have been lucky. In college, next to where our group practiced Karate, I found a secluded place in the university sports center where I built a home-made *maki-wara* from an aluminum tube and practiced on a regular basis. (I made sure my knuckles were more or less presentable

---

[126] The theory of the three *Ki* vectors is a lasting legacy of the late Sugiyama-sensei's tireless research for the advancement of Karate.

[127] Master Funakoshi, *My Way of Life* (cited at note 14) at 118, 119 – 20.

for my next day's class attendance.) Upon graduation, I built one in my basement. Upon arrival in Tokyo, one of my kind teachers built a *maki-wara* outside his *dōjō* because I had complained we did not have one. More than that, he got hold of a bunch of straw and together we plaited several *makiwara*. I got one extra and carried it with me whenever I would leave Tokyo on business or vacation.

Ideally, I want to strike *maki-wara* everyday. In practice, I find it difficult. Recently, I have tried to allocate one day a week when I strike *maki-wara* 1,000 times with my left hand and 500 times with the other. On other days, I do as much as I can. Naturally, I complement my *maki-wara* training with regular Karate practice.

Becoming Weak to Be Strong, or How to Make a Punch

> *"You must," I tell them, "become not strong but weak." ... "I want you to find the answers within yourselves," I tell them. "And I promise you that the time will come when you truly understand what I mean."*[128]
> —Master Funakoshi Gichin

Maki-wara practice consists of constant stimulation of *tanden* to produce strong *kime*. Its essence is activation and release of *Ki* accumulated primarily in *tanden* and the striking arm onto the target. If we think that the goal of striking the *maki-wara* is to develop calluses we miss the point. If we start practicing by using too much power, again, we slow ourselves down. Our punches will not be Karate punches and we won't be able to generate much *kime*. Striking like that against a real opponent might allow them to build defenses against the penetration of the *Ki* we thus deploy. Our goal is to eliminate all muscular force in the striking hand. Believe it or not, the "force" will magically appear of its own accord at the moment of impact. Remember, softness generates hardness and in turn hardness gives way to softness.

---

[128] Master Funakoshi, *My Way of Life* (cited in note 14) at 114.

Beyond the Outer Show of Strength – Forging *Ki* Channels

Techniques occur when void is encountered.[129]

—Master Funakoshi Gichin
(One of the Important Phrases of Karate)

I sometimes see beginners and more advanced students pounding on *maki-wara* by exerting all their physical strength, seeking the most re-sounding effect upon impact. Perhaps some of them look at *maki-wara* as their personal enemies to be crushed and broken to pieces. This kind of punching looks like a dynamic weight lifting exercise with the punching hand. With all the noise, the punch looks strong indeed.

Then I ask such a person to replicate his punch by striking me in the stomach. Usually, I feel almost no effect. The message: This kind of power-punch accomplishes little beyond giving the striking person a measure of self-satisfaction. This is not a Karate punch of today.

To produce the strongest *kime*, the movement just prior to impact must be devoid of any muscular force. *Tanden* is our power-plant to drive our movements. Imagine if you will that before impact you do not use any muscles. I know that this may go against the laws of modern physics. Just pretend that you have entered a Karate fantasy land where anything is possible.

Instead of deploying physical strength to move our striking fist, our minds alone – through activation of *Ki* – must deliver our punches to the target. To the venerable Sugiyama-sensei, the mind (*shin*) acts as a general who, always of tranquil disposition, controls his soldiers (*Ki*), who manifest their powers (*ryoku*) through the execution of physical techniques.[130]

The key is to gain facility to channel *Ki* through our bones and joints. Of course, our striking hand is fully energized, full of Yang *Ki* ready to be released – it is our *iki-te*. To my way of thinking, a repeated *maki-wara* practice helps forge new channels for *Ki* to flow from our *tanden* through our bodies (and bones), ending in the area of two knuckles with which we connect to the target.

---

[129] Master Funakoshi, *Karate Jutsu* (cited in note 15) at 175.
[130] Sugiyama-sensei, *11 Innovations* (cited in note 2) at 6.

Ideally, a punch is released of its own accord. Whenever a Yin vessel (an opening) is encountered, we can fill it in naturally and without hesitation with our Yang *Ki*. Like an arrow from a fully extended bow our moving arm shoots out stored *Ki*, closing the open space. In reality, our mind (consciously or not) ignites stored *Ki* into action by sending additional *Ki* impulse. Once triggered, the punch is guided to its intended destination by an automatic pilot.

Continuing to use muscular strength of the striking arm is, to paraphrase the venerable Sugiyama-sensei, like using First World War weaponry against cyberspace attacks. Our punches may look strong but their effect is often dubious. They are heavy and relatively slow. Granted, they may inflict much pain and damage, but they are unlikely to penetrate deep into the target. For an effective *kime* we try to use only *Ki* to propel our punches. No, we MUST use only *Ki*. Otherwise the practice makes no sense. It's a waste of time and equipment.[131]

From Weakness to Strength

Whenever [Motobu Choki-sensei] engaged opponents that were bigger or stronger than him, the master said he felt empowered by them.[132]
—Marukawa Kenji

Yesterday, I saw a beginner pounding mercilessly on *maki-wara*. I asked him to join me in *yakusoku kumite*. Using all the physical strength at his disposal, he could not block any of my punches. On the other hand, my blocks – initiated with no visible physical strength – effortlessly deflected his power punches away.

Listening to the *ki-sei* theory of hands, it seemed like a new world of Karate opened up before him. Scales seemed to fall from his eyes. I am curious to see if he follows up on his initial enchantment.

Like in Judo, so in Karate; we can gather our partners' physical strength and use it against them. Suddenly their physical strength or size

---

[131] I suppose that to those not familiar with *Ki*, moving our bodies by *Ki* alone might be equivalent to moving our bodies purely by will power.

[132] Marukawa Kenji, *Talking about My Teacher* (Patrick & Yuriko McCarthy trans.), quoted in Motobu-sensei, *Watashi no Karate-jutsu* (cited in note 17) at 29.

no longer matters – their strength can be our strength. Evidently, Motobu Choki-sensei (who "felt empowered" by his opponents) made good use of this principle.

Similarly, delivering attacks by moving attacking hands with *Ki* alone dispenses with physical strength. The "weaker" the hands, the more unstoppable, the more indefensible the attacks. If *Ki* alone transports our fists, seemingly there is nothing to defend against.

Total *Kime:* Focused Synchronization of Movement

At the instant of *kime*, all our energies zero in on the target. Our goal is to mobilize all the *Ki* at our disposal while guarding against any potential dissipation of energy.

We initiate and end our punches with a strong exhale from *tanden*. At the time of impact – the moment of *kime* – we contract and focus our entire mind and body toward the target without losing our *tanden*-located center. We evenly tighten up and contract our lower back, armpits and chest muscles to maintain strong connection with the rest of our body. Our buttocks are locked in. If we overextend our striking arm, we lose much of this connection and our *kime* suffers. Let's leave the practice of overextending striking arms to sports enthusiasts to whom genuine *kime* may be of lesser interest.

The Why of *Tanden*

We should have a strong sensation in our *tanden* – our distributor of *Ki*. Our intention to strike activates several streams of *Ki*. One stream empowers both our striking-hand and eye vectors – think of this pillar of *Ki* as an iron rod of energy, or the trunk of a powerful tree. Another stream flows from our *tanden* in the opponent's direction. Still another stream pushes down our legs. With *Ki* traveling in opposite directions at the moment of impact, we experience a tearing-apart feeling in our *tanden*.

The contraction of the small of our backs should coincide with the execution of our punch. Its contraction with an accompanying exhale determines the strength and sharpness of our *kime*.

In a word, *tanden* governs the delivery of our punches. It is an execution center. It is in charge of synchronizing all constituent actions with utmost speed, bearing all accompanying pressures. We must do all we can to nourish and cultivate its powers.

The Why of Stances

> There are no stances such as neko-ashi, zen-kutsu or kō-kutsu in my Karate. Neko-ashi is a form of "floating foot" which is considered very bad in bujutsu. If one receives a body strike, one will be thrown off balance. Zen-kutsu and kō-kutsu are unnatural, and prevent free footwork.[133]

—Motobu Choki-sensei

To make a punch against a striking post, we extend our *mete/ki* hand a little above our front knee while placing the *iki-te/sei* hand in a *hiki-te* position. Our bodies, sinews and bones are *Ki*-energized, our *tanden* full. We strike, slightly rotating – or, rather, shifting – our hips, punching *gyaku-zuki*, assuming one of several available stances, whose primary purpose is to facilitate contraction of the lower back while squeezing our inner thighs to further power and sharpen our *kime*.

I divide stances into three groups.[134]

Group 1. Stances in which my techniques are supported more or less evenly by both hips, legs and feet. These include *kiba-dachi*, *shiko-dachi*, *hachiji-dachi*, *heikō-dachi*, *san-chin-dachi*, and *hangetsu-dachi*.

Group 2. Stances in which I support my techniques mainly with the back hip, leg and foot, as my weight shifts toward the back leg. These include *kō-kutsu-dachi*, *fudo-dachi* (although some might not agree with this), *neko-ashi-dachi*, *re-no-ji-dachi*, and, if techniques are executed diagonally or to the side, also stances of Group 1, such as *kiba-dachi*, *heikō-dachi*, or *hachi-ji-dachi*.

Group 3. Stances in which I support my techniques with the front

---

[133] Nakata, *Collection of Sayings* (cited in note 85), quoted in Motobu-sensei, *Watashi no Karate-jutsu* (cited in note 17) at 32.

[134] For a comprehensive discussion of Karate stances refer to Nakayama Masatoshi-sensei's *Dynamic Karate: Instruction by the Master* 26 – 56 (Herman Kauz trans., Kodansha 1986) ("*Dynamic Karate*").

hip, leg and foot, including *zen-kutsu-dachi*, as my weight shifts toward the front leg.

To boost the discharge of *Ki* from *tanden* during *maki-wara* practice I lower my stance slightly, typically in a *hanmi* position, in order to lower my center of gravity, sinking my *Ki* toward *tanden* while preventing its dispersion in undesired directions. I normally strike *maki-wara* either from a front- or back-supporting-leg stance resembling *kiba-dachi*, sending *Ki* through *maki-wara* as well as downward through my supporting foot. I strongly grip the floor with both feet. On occasion, I also practice punching *maki-wara* in other stances, for example standing in *hachi-ji-dachi*, *kō-kutsu-dachi*, or regular *zen-kutsu-dachi*. In fact, I think of *kō-kutsu-dachi* and *zen-kutsu-dachi* as variations of the *kiba-dachi* stance with the body weight shifted backward or forward, respectively.

Stances should give us strong support for sending *Ki* to the floor through the soles of our feet. The idea is similar to the mechanics of jumping, where in order to jump we first exert pressure downward with our feet.[135] *Ki* sent down our legs and feet rebounds with *Ki* flowing in the opposite direction toward our *tanden*. For stronger contraction, I never fully straighten my back leg in Group 3 stances. Doing so might even lead to spinal injuries, as I have sometimes been warned.

Years ago, an instructor suggested that we make our front stances narrower – making almost one line with our feet, quite similar to the front stances demonstrated by Master Funakoshi in his *Karate Jutsu*. I followed that recommendation for some time but, because the teacher never explained the reason, I soon forgot about it, reverting to wider stances as they are generally practiced today.

Knowing the "why" changes our practice. Without knowing the reason, we tend to forget the proper form, just following the crowd. Knowing the "why," we practice with an ideal form in the back of our minds. This empowers and energizes our techniques. The perfect form, projected in our mind, subconsciously works toward its eventual realization.

Besides narrowing our stances, we can maximize *kime* by making them shorter. With shorter stances, contracting the small of our backs, our buttocks and the pulling together of inner thighs will be more

---

[135] I will elaborate on this idea in section on *tsukuri* later in this book.

effective – in fact while striking I have a distinct feeling of bringing both my hips together.

In the existing photographs, the distance between Master Funakoshi's feet is about shoulders' width. Saying that in older times people could not make longer stances is a rationalization. Of course they could. And they knew better not to.

While on the subject, I used to wonder about the best angle of the back foot in a front stance. Answers I received varied from teacher to teacher. Some even recommended making our feet parallel with each other facing the line of movement. As always, answers will depend on the questions we ask. Which position will squeeze our thighs more effectively? Which position can close in our buttocks tighter? I think the position with our back foot at 90° from the direction of our front stance – just as depicted by Master Funakoshi in his textbooks – is best. What do you think?

The Why of Fists

The Fist Is Instant Breath (Ken wa Shun-soku)
—Sugiyama Shojiro-sensei

We can deliver effective punches and strikes using a variety of open- and closed-hand configurations. We send *Ki* onto the target mostly with open or clenched hands. There is a *Ki* outlet in the middle of our palms called *lao-gong* (or *rō-kyū* in Japanese), through which we can relatively easily emit *Ki*. As a minor *chakra*, *rō-kyū* facilitates *Ki* exchange with our partners.

Yet, a fist is the preferred form of hand for a Karate punch. The reason: At impact we want to turn our punching hand into the hardest possible weapon to deliver its extreme Yang payload. The first two knuckles of our index and middle fingers are our Yang weapons of choice for delivery of maximum hardness.

Yin-and-Yang Fist Cycle

Our intention to deliver a punch creates a Yin *Ki* channel for its physical completion by our Yang-energized hand. From the ready-to-strike position until the hands return to their original place, our fists will have completed a full Yin-and-Yang cycle.

Yang *Iki-te* Hand. At the ready position, the punching *iki-te* hand is waiting at our hip in its incipient Yang state ready to send *Ki* away – <u>it is ready to give</u>. Its palm is facing up because on its way toward the hip it was in a Yin or receiving state just a moment ago, gathering *Ki*. It now rests there ready to strike, fully energized with Yang *Ki*.

Yin *Shini-te* Hand. Meanwhile, the other hand (it could be a hand that just finished a punch and exhausted its Yang energies) – extended forward above our knee – is in an incipient Yin state depleted of Yang *Ki* – <u>it is ready to receive</u>.

Completing the Cycle

The punching hand completes its Yang cycle upon completion of the punch, at which time its Yang reserves become spent. In its final stage of giving *Ki* away it assumed a Yang palm-down form. Simultaneously, the *shini-te* changes from its Yin condition back into an incipient Yang state as it gathers *Ki* along the way to the hip.

But wait, the hand that just delivered the punch is no longer active – it is now *shini-te*. Before that hand strikes again, it must change its condition to *iki-te*, filled with Yang *Ki* ready for action. It does this by moving gradually through the Yin palm-up form while gathering *Ki* until it transforms again to a Yang condition resting on our hip, ready to give, ready to strike.

To complete the full cycle we return to the original ready-to-strike position by bringing the fist that just completed the punch back to the hip while extending the other hand above the knee. By slightly brushing it with the other hand, as in a *ge-dan-barai* motion, we might help activate its *Ki* again by scooping *Ki* from the surface of the arm. Now this hand is again an *iki-te*, ready for the next strike. The cycle is complete.

Replenishing *Ki* in our body and *tanden* – we are not in a hurry – we repeat the striking sequence.

The palm-up palm-down changes in the fist's position reflect its Yin and Yang phases: In its Yin palm-up form the fist is naturally predisposed to receive *Ki*, while in its Yang palm-down form, the fist naturally gives or sends *Ki* away.

Forms of Fist

We can form *seiken, uraken* (back fist), *ken-tsui* (ulnar side of fist), *ippon-ken, nakadaka-ken,* or *hira-ken* (hand with four fingers bent at their second knuckles) – of closed-hand varieties, or we can form *shu-tō, hai-tō, haishu, nuki-te, tei-shō, sei-ryū-tō, kuma-de, keitō* (base of the thumb), or *washi-de* (fingers and thumb forming a bird's beak shape) – from among open-hand forms.[136] Although not exactly a hand form, the bent wrist of a hand (*kaku-tō*) can also be quite useful to block or attack.

But in *maki-wara* practice, we primarily use *seiken,* although we can occasionally use other forms of hand. Because there are no natural *Ki* outlets in the knuckles, we should practice forming *seiken* by striking *maki-wara* to open new *Ki* channels to let *Ki* flow through and between them.

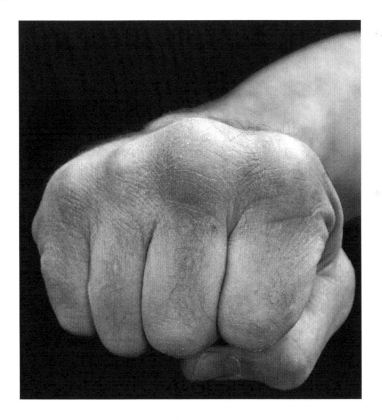

---

[136] For a thorough discussion of the use of hands in Karate, see Nakayama-sensei's *Dynamic Karate* (cited in note 134) at 74 – 83.

There are two methods of forming *seiken*. One way is to fold our small, ring, middle and index fingers and overlap them with the thumb. This is the only method I see in *dōjō* of today. It's the "all-fingers folded" fist.

Traditionally, we begin forming this type of fist by first folding the small finger and then the adjacent ones one by one. This way we can keep the small finger tightly clenched – a point of primary importance to many *Karate-ka*.[137] Without getting into the intricacies of meridian *Ki* pathways, I can say that while clenching the smaller finger, my neck naturally straightens and I feel stronger shoulder connection. Others, however, maintain that by beginning to clench fists with the index fingers, they can deliver more powerful blows. To learn the benefits or demerits of either method we should test both on an individual basis.

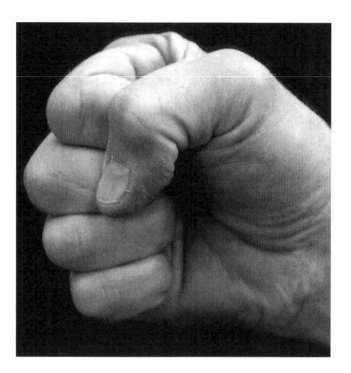

---

[137] In fact the Heart meridian ends its journey and the Small Intestine meridian begins its journey at the tip of the small finger. They combine as one of several Yin and Yang paired meridians. More interestingly, they both appear to extend to the area of lower *tanden*.

There is another method of forming *seiken* in which our extended index finger, after covering already clenched small, ring and middle fingers, is overlapped by the thumb – the "extended-index-finger" fist. This was a common form of fist in the past but it has now fallen into disuse.

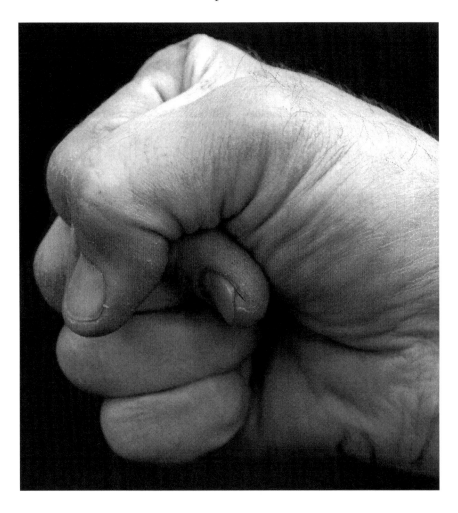

I have found, however, that choosing one type of *seiken* over the other is not just a matter of preference.

Question: *Keeping in mind previous lessons about the* iki-te-shini-te *and* ki-sei *role of hands, what possible benefit can you see in using the second* *("extended-index-finger") type of* seiken? *I will not answer this question for you. It is for you to discover.*

I have no "preference" for practicing *maki-wara* with either form of fist – I use them both, spending approximately equal time with each. For extra sharpness (*sae* in Japanese), I also strike *maki-wara* with *tate-ken* (vertical fist). The difference is that in using *seiken*, we twist our striking fists (not elbows) 180° at the final stage. Striking *tate-ken*, we twist them 90°. Naturally, there is no twisting in punching *ura-zuki*.

Maki-wara offers us opportunities to polish *kime* of other techniques, including back-fist (*ura-ken*), ridge-hand (*haitō*), knife-hand (*shu-tō*) or elbow (*enpi*)[138] strikes. Expanding the use of *maki-wara* beyond *seiken* punches will make us more versatile, allowing us to use a variety of techniques in the often unpredictable circumstances of life.

A more fundamental lesson for punching *maki-wara* with *seiken* is to keep our fists tightly clenched at the moment of impact. Since we propel our punches with *Ki* alone, it is easy to forget about it. The danger of injuries to our fists and wrists is obvious. Above all else, we clench our fists just before impact so that the *maki-wara* does not injure us.

Before and After *Kime*

> *Before one even begins his or her physical action, one extends one's Ki. We refer to this mental preparation as mind-before-impact. In short, one must <u>imagine the successful completion before the action</u>.*[139]
> —Sugiyama Shojiro-sensei

At the time of impact with *maki-wara*, the striking hand does not have to be extended all the way. Our intention should have already created a channel for the movement of the hand. In other words, our punch is

---

[138] The term *"enpi"* here refers to both an elbow (also referred to as *hiji*) and various elbow strikes. The term is written as 猿臂, with the first component meaning "monkey" and the other being an alternative kanji denoting an "elbow." The term should not be confused with *Enpi* Kata, where *Enpi* is written with characters denoting a flying swallow.

[139] Sugiyama-sensei, *11 Innovations* (cited in note 2) at 34.

already completed (in our mind) before the physical motion takes place. The rest is just finalizing the technique which can be broken down in two stages: First, carrying out the "physical action" ending with *kime* (synchronized focus of body and mind); second, following its completion (the impact) by momentarily maintaining *kime* and continuing the flow of *Ki* onto the target – a concept referred to as *zanshin*. To accomplish it and add teeth to the sustained flow of *Ki*, we double up the contraction of our *tanden*. (Of course, in sports Karate the concept of *zanshin* is meaningless.)

The late Sugiyama-sensei, to whom there was no Karate without *zanshin*,[140] gave us an apt example of *zanshin* closely related to the *Ki*-propelled way of striking. When at a shooting range, he asked his students to mentally connect and touch the target with the barrels of their pistols by imaging them to be 50 feet long and projecting *Ki* through them. He also asked them to continue *Ki* projection even after pulling the trigger. Amazingly, even people without prior experience hit the distant target accurately on the first day of practice.[141]

To explain how to strike is fairly easy: First we collect *Ki* in our *tanden*, sinews and bones which we then release onto the target, fully contracting our bodies and finishing all action at the same time. However, to actually execute an effective strike takes years of dedicated practice.

Turbocharging and Triggering Release of *Ki*

We practice with *maki-wara* to deliver *Ki* through our fists (or other parts of our bodies) in the most concentrated laser-like fashion. We already know that we can sharpen our *kime* by a simultaneous contraction of our body, squeezing our lower back, inner thighs and buttocks, and pressing down on our supporting leg. At first, however, our *kime* may be weak. Luckily, there are effective methods to turbocharge the release of *Ki* onto the target in pursuit of perfect *kime*.

---

[140] *Ibid.*

[141] *See ibid.* at 11.

The Why of *Ibuki*

*In Karate, **ibuki** is the most important thing to learn.*[142]

—Sugiyama Shojiro-sensei

Initiating strikes with a forceful exhale powers up our *kime*. We call this sudden *tanden*-generated spurt of air *ibuki*. Its role is to pressure our *tanden* and inject extra *Ki* into our techniques. Because the peak of *ibuki* coincides with the impact of a punch and the completion of all physical action, we may say that the punching process starts and ends with *ibuki*.[143]

There is a variety of sounds that may accompany *ibuki*, with many *Karate-ka* using sounds of their own. Indeed, various sounds have different effect on our *tanden* and the quality of released *Ki*. The best thing is to experiment on an individual basis to discover their subtleties. Yet, for all their benefits, when striking *maki-wara*, our *ibuki* does not carry much sound. It's OK to emit little sounds, but it would be too exerting to emit loud *kiai* over hundreds of striking repetitions.

More important, by controlling the force and length of *ibuki*, we control the speed of our hands, and the strength and sharpness (*sae*) of our *kime*. The stronger the *ibuki*, the more powerful our techniques. The shorter it is, the sharper they become, the quicker their delivery, and the more concentrated our *kime*. As the venerable Sugiyama-sensei pointed out, to add speed to our punches we don't think in terms of quicker execution – this might add tension to our muscles, making our punches slower. Instead, we think of making our *ibuki* shorter.[144].

The Why of Body Contraction

Upon completion of a technique, muscles should be evenly contracted. Both left and right side muscles as well as front and back muscles should be contracted with even tension.[145]

—Sugiyama Shojiro-sensei

---

[142] Ibid., 32.
[143] See ibid., 7.
[144] See ibid., 20.
[145] Ibid., 80.

At the moment of impact, all elements that make for the execution of an effective strike synchronize into one united whole. Our mental energy (*Ki*), our fists (*ken*), and our bodies (*tai*) fuse momentarily into oneness to produce the most powerful *kime*.

If our bodies are not fully contracted, we will not be able to use all the *Ki* at our disposal, some of which will dissipate in various directions or fail to be released. Moreover, a full contraction of our bodies will protect against an unwelcome rebound of our punching arm upon impact.

Easier said than done. That's why we focus on contracting our minds and those parts of our bodies that are most critical to produce effective *kime*. Focusing on a powerful contraction of the small of our backs will result in the contraction of our abdominal muscles and exert extra pressure on *tanden*. As Sugiyama-sensei taught, we "pull our sacrum (tailbone) upward and try to push the solar plexus against it."[146]

This contraction will send an impulse of *Ki* through the three vectors of *kime*. A gentle contraction of our genital muscles and inner thighs will seal the critical *ein* acupuncture point[147] to prevent dispersion of *Ki* through it. At the same time, we contract and merge our entire bodies, especially our armpits, into one unified whole. Pushing our shoulders down will secure and solidify this contracting action. We help squeeze our *tanden* – which moves up slightly at the time of *kime* – by squeezing our buttocks and inner thighs, while extending and pushing our sacrum forward and up.

Finally, upon impact, we strive at a full symmetrical contraction of our armpits and chest muscles – no overextending of our arms. That way, the overall contraction of our bodies is at its strongest.

To produce the strongest *kime* as a result of the total contraction of our bodies, we maintain a state of total relaxation from the moment of initiation of our techniques until the moment of impact. Otherwise, our *kime* will suffer, our techniques will markedly slow down, and we won't be able to fully mobilize all the *Ki* at our disposal.

---

[146] *See ibid.*, 21.

[147] This point is referred to as *hui-yīn* in Chinese and "Meeting of Yin" in English.

The Why of *Hiki-te*

The hands should move without conscious thought.[148]
—Fifth of the eight precepts of Chuan Fa

To accelerate *Ki* release, we press both shoulders down, strongly pulling the non-striking hand diagonally downward (*hiki-te*). Yes, the role of *hiki-te* is to turbocharge the release of *Ki* – not to artificially overextend hips, torso, or the striking arm. The more *Ki* it collects along the way to the hip, the more *Ki* flows through our striking arm. Moreover our *hiki-te* helps pull our shoulder down, adding extra stimulus for the release of *Ki* from *tanden*. This "priming" of *tanden* by an independent *Ki* stream flowing down our spines further stimulates the release of *Ki* from *tanden*.

Question: *How can we help lower our shoulders? If you can answer this question without looking ahead in the text, you could probably make a good Karate instructor.*

An effective *hiki-te* will naturally be strongly connected to our torsos, the way we may have been taught when our instructors tried to pull our *hiki-te* away from our bodies to test our armpit contraction. Doing so, we seal several energy points around our armpits and rib cage to prevent *Ki* from leaking. Having sealed these points and energy points previously discussed, when we twist the fist of our *hiki-te* toward our torso, we automatically direct *Ki* to travel through the striking arm toward the target. In fact, I sometimes think of *hiki-te* as a trigger for the action of my other hand.

More fundamentally, *hiki-te* allows us to maintain a Yin-and-Yang balance and stability. As already mentioned, without fully Yang-energized *hiki-te*, we would become defenseless upon execution of a technique. To maintain such balance, our hands must work together as a single Yin-and-Yang unit.

---

[148] Quoted in Michael Clarke, *Shin Gi Tai: Karate Training for Body, Mind, and Spirit* 241 (YMAA Publication Center 2011); *see also* Eight Precepts of Quanfa in *Bubishi: The Classic Manual of Combat* 197 (translated with commentary by Patrick McCarthy, Tuttle 2008).

Properly aligned, the *hiki-te* vector always points at the opponent, or, while punching a *maki-wara*, the striking post. This is the ABC of Karate. As currently practiced, however, *hiki-te* is twisted sideways to the back of the body, pointing away from a potential target. I believe that this is a grave mistake, resulting from the lack of understanding of the principles of Ying and Yang. The reason for aligning *hiki-te* with the potential target is to make it always available to seize upon an opening by delivery of a straight punch in the shortest and most rapid way. If our *hiki-te* is positioned sideways, pointing away from the target, our punches will have to take a circular course to reach their destination. Well and good for *mawashi-* or *furi-zuki* but cumbersome for a straight punch.

As demonstrated in Master Funakoshi's Kata positions in *Karate Jutsu*, *hiki-te* typically faces the line of potential attack. Evidently, the ancients knew the Yin-and-Yang principles. They knew that *hiki-te* is a ready position to be released of its own accord once an opening is created or perceived.

Explanations given for artificially twisting *hiki-te* make little sense. Some say that *hiki-te* twists together with the hips and follows them to a *hanmi* position. But why should it? If we are to punch while rotating our hips into the *shōmen* position, wouldn't our *hiki-te* fists have to follow a circular trajectory as well?

Another explanation is that twisting *hiki-te* backward is just for practice. Practice of what? In *Budō* everything we do is for real. Mistakes learned during practice will reflect later in applications of techniques. There are no second chances. Now is now. The future may never arrive.

Moreover, artificially pulling *hiki-te* to the back sacrifices a solid contraction of our armpits. This is unpardonable. Open armpits create undesirable escape routes for *Ki*, depleting it from our techniques. Watching students practicing with space gaping between their elbows and bodies, or between their back hands and trunks in *shu-tō-uke*, I feel like crying.

We don't need excuses for – or justifications of – incorrect forms. We need to critically analyze our techniques to make them most effective. Let's not sacrifice the multiple benefits of *hiki-te* aimed at the target for some illusory benefits of meaningless and pseudo-functional forms.

Admittedly, outside of *maki-wara* and *kumite* training, the role of *hiki-te* could be to pull and twist the opponent's attacking hand to throw them off balance.[149] Another application could be to pull the opponent toward us at the time of delivery of a strike, doubling its power upon impact.[150] But even in these applications our *hiki-te* must be ready for the next possible action.

The Why of *Fumi-komi*

> *Stomp the floor with the entire mass of your body. If you stomp with only your foot, your punch will be weak.*[151]
>
> —Sugiyama Shojiro-sensei

Similar in function to an explosive *ibuki*, *fumi-komi* – forcefully stomping the floor with our supporting leg (*sasae-ashi*) upon impact – will supercharge the release of *Ki*, adding strength to our punch. To accelerate the movement of *Ki* toward the target, paradoxically we strongly press with our feet onto the floor with the mass of our entire bodies. Puzzling indeed.

On closer analysis, the mystery dissolves. Pushing the floor with the sole of the foot of our supporting leg creates a rebound of *Ki* from the floor which supercharges the *Ki* we send toward the opponent from our *tanden*, our striking arm and our eyes, multiplying the strength of our *kime*.

Years ago, I used to apply *fumi-komi* on a regular basis while striking *maki-wara*. Nowadays, I sometimes see it in everyday sparring. I believe that we could make even better use of it by regularly employing it in *kihon* or *kumite* practice.

The Why of Twisting Fists

A sudden synchronized turn of both fists in a corkscrew fashion strengthens and accelerates *tanden* and body contraction, and boosts the flow of *Ki* through our spine. The body connection solidifies. The mutual

---

[149] *See* Master Funakoshi, *Karate Jutsu* (cited in note 15) at 48.

[150] *See, e.g.*, Master Funakoshi, *Kyōhan* (cited in note 6) at 22 and *Karate Jutsu* (cited in note 15) at 95 ("This type of technique of grabbing any part of the opponent and pulling him into the punch utilizes the opponent's energy and thus doubles the effect of the punch.").

[151] Sugiyama-sensei, *11 Innovations* (cited in note 2) at 164.

transmutation of Yin-Yang energies of hands comes naturally. *Ki* leaking points along our torso are sealed. *Kime* magnifies.

For maximum contraction we twist our fists, not our elbows. In fact, watching Karate experts, I often see that the elbows of their striking arms do not change at all during the twisting motion.

Why is it that a regular straight punch (*choku-zuki*) and *tate-ken-zuki* end up with striking fists twisted, but *ura-zuki* does not? The best I can say is that *ura-zuki* is not a complete punch. We apply it out of necessity. It is used when the distance does not allow us to develop a fully extended punch. Naturally, given a choice, we want to extend our punches upon impact to take full advantage of the extra spiking effect of twisting fists.

Nonetheless, there is more to *ura-zuki* than an incomplete straight punch. It has a legitimate application when the course of the punch is circular, similar to an uppercut in boxing, and even some Kata appear to feature this technique. But let's not jump to conclusions. Could this motion's alternate (if not primary) function be to disentangle ourselves from our opponent's holds, or penetrate with our hands into their bodies in preparation for possible throwing or choking techniques or take-downs?

The Why of *Me-sen*

> *Me-sen is a fundamental component of Karate for delivering shocking power to the target.*[152]
>
> —Sugiyama Shojiro-sensei

I learned the power of an eye vector performing the "unbendable-arm" exercise with the venerable Sugiyama-sensei.[153] In this exercise, a person extends an arm with an open hand, placing its wrist on the shoulder of another person, who then tries to bend that arm at the elbow with their arms. The answer to sensei's tricky question, "How do you disarm the partner's iron-like extended arm?" exposes the underlying principle of *me-sen*'s invisible power.

---

[152] Sugiyama-sensei, *11 Innovations* (cited in note 2) at 18.
[153] *See ibid.*

Question: *Can you answer that question yourself?*

So far, I have discussed two main streams of *Ki* projection – one flowing through our arms, the other from our *tanden*. Enter the eye-vector, or *me-sen* – the third power vector along which we project *Ki* through our eyes. Interestingly, many powerful people – in and outside Karate – have either developed or been gifted with powerfully piercing eyes, perhaps giving us an inkling to their powers of focus and concentration. Recall, for instance, the story of Bushi Matsumura Sōkon whose fierce glare had a paralyzing effect on his challenger.

Luckily, we can cultivate the *Ki* power emanating from our eyes. We can even look with our eyes through our own or our partners' bodies. A few exercises to nurture the power of *me-sen* are shown in the late Sugiyama-sensei's textbook.[154]

Vision is of primary importance in Karate. Normally we never look straight at oncoming attacks or our sparring partners. Looking straight in the eyes of a strong opponent courts an early defeat by allowing their *Ki* to enter and overpower us through our eyes. Looking straight at an opponent, we also miss most of what happens around us – our vision narrows and our reactions to their incipient motions slow down. Yet, direct vision is all I see in an average *dōjō*. It may be OK in business interactions, but has no place in *Budō*.

Instead, we use our peripheral vision, which maximizes our perception, particularly in *kumite* practice. The mechanics of peripheral vision are well explained in Sugiyama-sensei's textbook.[155]

However, at the moment of *kime* of our attack we refocus the *Ki* flowing from our eyes, looking straight through the target, converging our *me-sen* with *Ki* vectors of our striking hand and our *tanden* at a distance of approximately 100 feet. This letting out of a stream of *Ki* through our eyes is not unlike breathing out through them. Zeroing in on the three *Ki* vectors at that point will produce an optimal *kime* at the moment of impact.[156]

---

[154] *Ibid.*, 227 – 28.

[155] *Ibid.*, 37.

[156] The concept of meeting the *tanden*, arm and eye vectors was developed by the venerable Sugiyama-sensei. *See* Sugiyama-sensei, *11 Innovations* (cited at 2) at 19 & 80.

The Why and Why Not of Hip Rotation

Because it is often said that we initiate punches from our hips, some might jump to the conclusion that hip rotation adds horsepower to our punches, making them faster.

Let's start with the mechanics of movement. When stepping forward or backward, our legs do not follow a straight course – they follow a some-what zigzag, semi-circular path. In midcourse, our thighs pull toward each other with knees almost touching. This mutual pull of inner thighs momentarily squeezes our buttocks, exerting extra pressure on our ab-dominal muscles and adding extra impulse of *Ki* to our techniques. More important, the contraction of these muscles, including our genital mus-cles, closes the acupoint located along the perineum, which is called the "Meeting of Yin" place (*ein* in Japanese), preventing unwanted escape of *Ki*.

In the same fashion, in a stationary strike, we complete our action by squeezing our buttocks and inner thighs. We do so regardless of whether we strike from a back-leg-supported, front-leg-supported, or both-feet-supported stance. This contraction adds extra zing to our *kime*.

Orthodox teachings, however, emphasize hip rotation. In fact, I often see practitioners overly extending their hips in a *hanmi* position, often losing their thigh-to-thigh connection. They believe that such hip rota-tion will increase the speed of a punch. Perhaps, but the physical motion of rotation takes too much time. If we were to deliver a cannon ball, the running start achieved by such action might be justified. But our goal is not to power a physical action. It is to deliver a *Ki* impulse. There is no time to waste on redundant physical motions. The wider the hip rotation, the more time it takes to punch.

Rather than maximizing physical speed with muscular strength, we look for an instantaneous delivery of *Ki* impulse through the body of the opponent. If we were to deliver a cannon ball with our hand, a large hip rotation might add momentum before its release – but we aren't. We are looking for a split-second activation of *tanden* for an instant release of *Ki* through the target. Toward that end, a slight (but only slight) rotation or vibration of hips may indeed be helpful.

Hip rotation, to the extent it activates *Ki* in our *tanden* is helpful;

doing it to propel an imaginary "cannon ball" to the target is a misguided action. Just a slight shift of the hips is ideal – indeed, calling this movement a "rotation" seems to be a misnomer justifying unnecessary hip motion.

A little knowledge is sometimes more harmful than total ignorance. By overextending our hips, and worse, by overly twisting *hiki-te* to the back, we misdirect both *tanden* and the striking arm away from the potential target, making an effective *Ki*-based strike less likely.

Let's not forget that our strike must be completed before any physical action even begins. In other words, the Yin form of a punch precedes the physical action of filling it with the Yang of our hand. In case of a straight punch, we must therefore align the direction of *Ki* from our *tanden* and striking arm toward the target.

The mutual pull of our gluteal muscles and inner thighs while pointing the striking arm and *tanden* toward the target adds focus to our *kime*. A **slight shift** (without losing connection between our thighs) or vibration of hips will help activate *tanden*, turning it into an additional means of boosting *kime*.

The Why of Punching Distance

> *I still do not know the best way to punch the maki-wara.*[157]
>> —Motobu Choki-sensei (uttered while being
>> presumably over 60 years of age)

Why do we normally initiate *maki-wara* punches with fists resting at our hips? So positioned, our fists need to travel a long distance to the target. In actual encounters, however, this position may be unrealistic. Both hands must protect our body, ready to strike at any moment, however close the target may be. Restricting *maki-wara* training this way gives me pause: Is my practice for real, or, is it merely a source of dubious self-satisfaction?

Inspired by Motobu Choki-sensei's demonstration of shattering a wooden board hanging close to his striking fist, I now supplement my

---

[157] Motobu-sensei, *Watashi no Karate-jutsu* (cited in note 17) at 31.

maki-wara practice by punching from a short distance – a few inches away. I strike with either my leading or back hand, focusing on developing sharp *kime* comparable to striking from the hip. I believe that doing so brings my practice to a new level.

Striking this way, we can also get a deeper understanding of the role of *hiki-te*. Far from twisting it around our torsos or pulling our shoulders back, *hiki-te* helps rebalance the Yin-and-Yang equilibrium between our hands – becoming instantly Yang-*Ki* energized at the moment the other hand connects with the target. The distance it travels becomes of secondary importance. The exchange of Yin and Yang energies between hands is what matters.

The ability to produce instantaneous *kime* from any distance is the true test of our Karate ability. In it lies the secret of the art.

The Why of Imagery

The most effective punch will have little muscular strength behind it, as its power derives from a sudden release of *Ki* through our striking arm toward the target. To do so, we seal several energy points along our bodies to prevent unwanted escape of *Ki* by twisting our *hiki-te* and contracting other muscles. At the same time, by pushing out *Ki* with explosive *ibuki*, we leave it little room to travel anywhere other than along the striking arm. As we concentrate on our *hiki-te*, we practically forget about our striking arm – it will find its way toward the target on its own. Indeed, as explained before, when we strike, the punch has already been completed on a mental level. The imagery of what follows teleports our striking fist to the target with no physical action in between.

A Word of Caution

Incorrect *maki-wara* practice carries the danger of injury. The danger is especially real if we pound the striking post deploying our physical, muscular strength. By doing so, we can easily damage our hands, wrists, shoulders, spine, hips or other parts of our bodies. The pressures on our entire skeleton can be overwhelming, and can cause severe (and often lasting) damage and injuries to our bones, joints and cartilage. **I therefore urge anyone interested in pursuing *maki-wara* training to do so only under the direct supervision of a competent Karate instructor.**

CHAPTER 6
The Why of Blocking

> *In Karate, there is no advantage to be obtained in becoming an aggressor. It is important that one's first move be that of warding off an attack, even though in practice this defensive act will have the character of an attack in itself.*[158]
>
> —Master Funakoshi Gichin

Why Block?

A good question. A better way might be to attack as soon as we sense an imminent attack, stealing the wind of aggression from the opponent. An artful application of *mikiri* might be another solution. At this level of the art, a block might indeed appear useless – a fancy invention of Karate teachers to help them earn a living. At the highest level, of course, we can disarm the energy of aggression with the power of *Ki* alone, as discussed in "A *Ki* Master Class" section above. But there is more to *uke* than merely parrying or preempting an oncoming attack.

Blocking or Receiving?

Is *"uke"* just a "block"? Perhaps not.

The term *uke* comes from the Japanese verb *ukeru*, whose primary meaning is to "receive." Not block but receive. Perhaps the problem lies in the translation. Perhaps the problem lies in attaching limiting names to techniques. Anyway, faced with the threat of a powerful attack, Karate invites us to "receive" rather than "block" it. Frightening enough? While on the subject, how about "receiving" punches with our bodies? Indeed, Master Itosu reportedly could "receive" any attack with his body without any visible effect on him.

---

[158] Master Funakoshi, *Kyōhan* (cited in note 6) at 32.

I heard that Kata techniques originally carried no names. Then somebody decided to label them, calling some *uke* – for better or worse. Let's work with it and see if we can make some sense of blocks as "receiving" techniques.[159]

Ki-Receiving Blocks: Stealing the Opponent's *Ki*

Concept of *Hiraishin* (Lightning Conductor)

Through practice, we can develop skills to receive partners' attacks without fear or pain. The secret lies in projecting and receiving *Ki*. In *Ki*-receiving blocks, we don't resist the incoming power of *Ki* – we receive it.

Think of the blocking hand as a lightning rod (*hiraishin* in Japanese) receiving the *Ki* of attack, and the counter-attacking hand as projecting *Ki* toward the target. The receiving hand momentarily depletes the opponent's *Ki* leaving them vulnerable to a counter.

Talking about "receiving" blocks, I have developed a modified *age-uke* where the "receiving" hand first fully extends toward the opponent (as if in a punching motion) and then in a circular guiding motion catches a *jō-dan* attack, returning either to the orthodox finishing position of *age-uke* or grabbing the attacker's hand and continuing downward to imbalance them. The block does not bounce, push or slide aside the attack forward – it is a reverse motion catching up with, following and re-directing a strike. In the course of this block, I transfer the received energy to my other hand with which I can simultaneously counterattack (without the need to first pull that hand as *hiki-te*).[160]

A variation of this block could be used against *jō-dan shu-tō-uchi* attacks in a way similar to an alternate application of the opening "block" of *Kankū Dai*.

Nonetheless, if the course of the orthodox *age-uke* is correct, ie catching the opponent's arm at an angle while sliding it along in a forward

---

[159] A good compilation of blocking techniques can be found in Nakayama Masatoshi-sensei's *Dynamic Karate* (cited in note 134).

[160] The idea of this block came to me while studying *The Three Parries* section in *The Scroll of Water* of Miyamoto Musashi's *The Complete Book of Five Rings* 57 (Kenji Tokitsu ed. & trans., Shambhala 2010).

motion, such a block could also be a "receiving" block. What matters is the direction of *Ki* in our blocking hand.

Yes, we may reverse the flow of *Ki* in our hands as in the example of the hand serving as a lightning rod. In that case, the blocking hand received the opponent's *Ki*, while the other struck by using a continuous flow of energy. Think of the receiving hand as sucking the opponent's *Ki* toward your *tanden*. Ideally we want to receive and return *Ki* simultaneously, or at least make a block and counter one continuous motion.

We execute both blocking and counterattacking on an exhale (*ibuki*). Yes, we can direct the flow of *Ki* anyway we want on either exhale or inhale. Experiment and you'll find the way.

A word of caution. The amount of *Ki* we absorb through our blocking hand may prove inadequate to disarm a powerful attack. Worse, if our "receiving" hand happens to project (rather than receive) *Ki* toward the attacking hand, it may cause the opponent to react with even greater force and overpower our receiving intention. To avoid injury or getting hit, we may need to either sidestep (*tai-sabaki*) or sway our head out of reach of the coming attack. As the power of the *Ki* we command grows, our *Ki*-receiving blocks should prove more effective.

Other *Ki*-Receiving Blocks

Ki-neutralizing blocks are further examples of *Ki*-receiving blocks. In these blocks, we meet the hardness of attacks with the softness of our hands. Sometimes a mere touch of our hand will neutralize the hard *Ki* of an attack. For better effect, we may glide over the attacking hand to disarm the hardness of a powerful punch. Some people refer to these blocks as "pressing blocks" or *osae-uke*. By using that name, however, we may miss the mechanics of the block: We do not "press," we neutralize the opponent's hard *Ki* by the softness of ours.[161]

---

[161] Pressing blocks belong to the next-discussed Ki-projecting blocks category.

Ki-Projecting Blocks

Ki-receiving blocks are only a part of our blocking arsenal and "stealing the opponent's *Ki*" is not the aim of every block. By projecting *Ki* through our blocking limbs we can also effectively block incoming attacks.

Attacking Blocks

Rather than receiving the *Ki* of attacks, we can strike the attacking limbs by explosively projecting *Ki* through our forearms, fists, back-fists, fingers, elbows, or legs.[162] While such blocks will deflect strikes or kicks into a zone of safety, they will often inflict much pain, causing attackers to reconsider continuing aggression.

The essence of attacking blocks is to create a momentary state of *kyo* in the opponent. A hard, punishing hit on their attacking limbs tends to disrupt their flow of *Ki*, creating a perfect time for counter-action. The harder we hit, the deeper the *kyo* is likely to be.

Compared with *Ki*-receiving blocks, attacking blocks are hard-type blocks. Let's not get carried away however. In the past some people would not want to engage in *yakusoku kumite* with me because my blocks caused them excessive pain. In time, I managed to adjust the strength of my blocks to achieve just the desired effect of bouncing the attacks off.

Guiding Blocks

By projecting *Ki* through our blocking limbs and joining it with the *Ki* of an oncoming attack in the direction of the attacking force, we can redirect and deflect the attack. *Nagashi-uke* is one example of such a block. We can use our hands, forearms or shins to guide away oncoming attacks.

Another application of a *Ki*-guiding block is to "scoop" the attacking strike or kick. We call scooping-type blocks *sukui-uke*.

---

[162] *See* Master Funakoshi's discussion of striking blocks (*uchi-te*) in his *Karate Jutsu* (cited in note 15) at 48.

Pressing Blocks

Pressing blocks resemble attacking or *Ki*-neutralizing blocks but only on the outside. Indeed, both attacking *age-uke* and *ge-dan-barai* can become pressing blocks, in which case the *Ki* of the blocking hand merges with the *Ki* of the attacking hand. Together they exert gradual pressure on the attacking hand to shift its *Ki*-vector away from our body. *Maki-otoshi-uke* could also be considered an example of such a block. A swirling *ge-dan-barai* as practiced in *Gōjū-ryū* also belongs in this category.

Movement-Arresting Blocks

Movement-arresting blocks are of the *Ki*-projecting variety. We block by pressing into the opponent's elbow or leg (either with our elbow or our foot) to prevent the attack from continuing – stopping it in midcourse. We can even effectively stop an attack at its inception by pressing on the shoulder of the striking hand with the palm of our hand. The effect of such a block, when executed well, can be stunning on the opponent – stopping them momentarily in their tracks.

We might also find ourselves in situations where, unable to react otherwise, we can extend our arm to keep our opponent outside their *uchi-ma*. This obviously assumes that our arm is long enough.

Block and Counterattack Is One Technique

> *When spying an opening, instantly take advantage, and if the opponent flees, immediately pursue.*[163]
>
> —Master Funakoshi Gichin

Regardless whether we apply *Ki*-receiving or *Ki*-projecting blocks, we must either simultaneously or immediately thereafter follow with a counter. Without it, blocking is just half the story of Karate.

---

[163] *Ibid.*

What matters is applying a simultaneous flow of *Ki* in blocking and attacking. In *Ki*-receiving blocks we let *Ki* received through the blocking motion flow to our *tanden*, directing it toward our counterattacking hand for a powerful *kime*. In *Ki*-projecting blocks, we continue to project *Ki* toward both the blocking and counterattacking hands or legs. Physically, blocking and attacking may consist of two motions but the flow of *Ki* continues throughout the movement. To reiterate, just like during execution of any other technique, we always block on an exhale. Blocking on an inhale would be suicide.

I think that dividing blocks and counterattacks into two motions is incorrect. If, after finishing a block we embark on a separate technique, in effect we become the aggressors. Furthermore, if we separate the two motions, we will fail to use our opponent's attacking *Ki* – a concept central to many forms of *Budō*. As Master Funakoshi taught, there should be almost no time between blocking and counterattacking. According to the Master, "offense and defense are inherently related – inseparable even for an instant."[164]

---

[164] Master Funakoshi, *Karate Jutsu* (cited in note 15) at 36.

CHAPTER 7
The Why of Kata

In the past, it was expected that about three years were required to learn a single Kata, and it was usual that even an expert of considerable skill would only know three or at the most five Kata.[165]

—Master Funakoshi Gichin

From Start to Finish

It is safe to say that Karate begins and ends with Kata.[166]

—Master Funakoshi Gichin

Before Okinawan masters introduced Karate to Japan, learning Karate meant – in addition to *maki-wara* practice – learning Kata. Far from mindlessly repeating the prescribed sequences of motion, the exercise aimed at bringing to life the cryptic Kata movements by searching for and applying their meanings in simulated combat situations. Instruction was one-on-one. Nobody got rich. Karate was a way of life, a part of Okinawa culture. Karate was Kata. Kata was Karate.

Once Upon a Time

In the purposely unrecorded times of early Karate history, a few enthusiasts of weaponless fighting busied themselves with improving old techniques and searching for new ones. Soon, the techniques multiplied, their variations too many to keep count of. But, "How to catalogue them?;" "How to preserve them for future generations?," they wondered. Of course, "Let's arrange them thematically in sequential clusters of

---

[165] Master Funakoshi, *Kyōhan* (cited in note 6) at 38.
[166] Master Funakoshi, *Essence* (cited in note 1) at 101.

movement not unlike musical compositions," they agreed. A concept of Kata was born.

Since the techniques were secret, not to be revealed to uninvited eyes, they encrypted them in a code that only they could understand. Thus the recorded movements would be gobbledygook to the outside world; as impenetrable as an obscure language.

Today, with Kata external movements lifted from secrecy, few *Karate-ka* have recognized the obvious truth: that Kata do not reveal techniques explicitly. Patrick McCarthy-sensei is one of the few who took a fresh look at Kata only to be stricken by the *blinding flash of the obvious*, as he put it. Of course, Kata cannot be taken literally; they are just mnemonics for remembering hidden techniques which, after decoding, should be practiced in two-person drills (or *futari-geiko* (二人稽古)) that show how to respond to simulated real-life acts of violence.[167]

Learning Kata – Unraveling the Code

From ancient times, an aura of sanctity attached to Kata, their movements never to be changed, altered or tinkered with. As someone has said, Kata are not things. They are not mere repositories of lifeless, mechanical techniques. They are alive, filled with the spirit of their creators, endowed with the soul of *Budō* which we animate when restoring the concealed techniques back to life. All we have to do is "reverse-engineer" the secret templates of techniques – to borrow McCarthy-sensei's terminology – and replace mindless solitary repetitions of abstract movements with full-blown two-person practice of techniques designed for real-life situations.[168]

Without such reverse-engineering, repeating Kata movements in their encrypted form is like repeating a script written in an unknown foreign language. We may repeat it a hundred, a thousand, or a million times, and still remain none the wiser. It does not matter if we modify Kata's particular steps, tweaking movements here and there – it continues

---

[167] *See* Patrick McCarthy-sensei, *Sometimes you don't know how to fit in until you break out* (2005); http://www.koryu-uchinadi.org/KU_HAPV.pdf (visited June 28, 2017).
[168] *See ibid.*

to be incomprehensible mumbo-jumbo no matter how we spell its particular words.

Learning Karate has been compared with learning a foreign language, and sparring with a partner to verbal dialogue.[169] I wish I could learn a foreign language without understanding the meaning of its words and engage in stimulating conversations on any topic. Perhaps robots of the future will do it – I can't. We call such meaningless talk "nonsense."

If mastery of a single Kata took three years in olden days, it is now common to earn the first black belt (entailing the "knowledge" of all basic Kata) within three years. Equipped with this emblem of achievement, many slump in their effort to improve, thinking they already know it all. In truth, they know only the outward forms of movement of several Kata, which they repeat oblivious of their significance. Sadly, they know very little.

If we can memorize the movements of any Kata in a month or so, then, "What on earth were the older generations doing for three long years while working on a single Kata?," one might ask. Could it be that they were deciphering the encrypted movements within Kata and reenacting them in drills resembling potential real-life encounters?

Repeating the shorthand transcription of Kata techniques exactly as handed down to us is just that: repeating a shorthand catalogue of techniques, not the techniques themselves. Yet, rehearsing such shorthand transcription for its own sake – not as a way of decrypting the true meaning – is all I see in a typical *dōjō*. Why can't we see the absurdity of equating these shorthand notations with real techniques?

Repeating the shorthand of Kata movements even a gazillion times

---

[169] *See, e.g.,* Sugiyama-sensei, *11 Innovations* (cited in note 2) at 12 (comparing various elements of Karate to phonetics (ability to relax and tense), articulation and pronunciation (sharpness and speed of techniques), memorizing words (basic techniques), good grammar (strategy), conversation and written communication (competition-type sparring)); McCarthy-sensei, *Putting the Fight back in Kata* ("How many times have you learned a Kata, but had no idea what offensive themes its defensive principles actually addressed? Or, that such themes even existed! It's a common problem that's been compared to learning a song in a foreign language. Melodic, but if you can't speak the language, the meaning of the song's words remains a total mystery! When you learn a Kata without knowing about its inner workings, you might as well be dancing."), http://www.ikkf.org/article3Q00.html (visited June 28, 2017).

will not advance our knowledge of it. For that, after cracking the code, we must practice each Kata technique in two-person drills (as advocated by McCarthy-sensei) for a minimum of three years. Then, we may say we have mastered it.

Practicing with Awareness

> *You may train for a long, long time, but if you merely move your hands and feet and jump up and down like a puppet, learning Karate is not very different from learning to dance. You will never have reached the heart of the matter; you will have failed to grasp the quintessence of Karate-dō.*[170]

—Master Funakoshi Gichin

Some *dōjō* stress the beauty of Kata movements. Well and good. The beauty of form is said to give rise to stronger, purer *Ki*. But ending there consigns Kata to be little more than a well-choreographed dance performance or beauty pageant.

Practicing Real Techniques, Not Their Encryptions

Our challenge is to distill from each mnemonic element of Kata the fullness of its underlying technique. Our challenge is to find those hidden techniques, interpret the foreign language of Kata, and make our practice realistic. Unless we know the meaning of each Kata move, its practice is meaningless, as "knowledge of just the sequence of a form is useless."[171] Needless to say, we practice Kata by applying their hidden techniques together with partners.

Don't Ask; Don't Tell

One thing gives me pause. If the old Okinawan masters knew the meanings of Kata movements, why didn't they transmit them to their students?

---

[170] Master Funakoshi, *My Way of Life* (cited in note 14) at 105.
[171] Master Funakoshi, *Kyōhan* (cited in note 6) at 39.

Maybe, if handed the meanings on a silver platter, students would have little incentive to search on their own. They might never advance far along The Way. Leaving the meanings hidden, on the other hand, offered sincere students an inducement to progress by probing for answers on their own.

Most students, however, do not ask questions. They follow Kata blindly. Over the past 40 years I can only recall one single occasion when a Karate practitioner asked me about the meaning of a certain movement in a Kata. That's all.

Waiting for the meanings of techniques to magically appear on the screens of our minds is an exercise in futility. Regardless of the number of repetitions – 100, 1,000, or 10,000 – their meanings will not jump at us on their own. Worse, they will recede further into oblivion. I am still waiting for some Karate veteran to prove me wrong.

This Is What Happened

A more plausible explanation is that even the masters didn't know – their teachers never told them. They learned simply by imitating the original movements. If they knew the meanings, they discovered them through their own efforts, by asking questions and finding answers. If at first teachers transmitted Kata's inner knowledge orally to a selected few, by the time Karate went public, this oral tradition (*kuden*) was apparently gone.[172]

I'll tell you what happened. The early Okinawan pioneers of the art, such as Tōde-Sakugawa (Sakugawa "Chinese Hands"),[173] travelled to China in search of genuine Karate teachers. Naturally, nobody would teach those strangers the secret art that was religiously guarded from outsiders over generations. Still, the visitors insisted, not taking "no"

---

[172] With the introduction of Karate into public schools, Okinawan masters may have deliberately suppressed transmission of oral traditions of Kata *bunkai*. Similarly, they might have been reluctant to teach the true meanings of Kata to the Japanese to the point of propagating incorrect and confusing meanings of techniques.

[173] *See Karate Dō Kyōhan: Master Text for the Way of the Empty-Hand* 7 (Harumi Suzuki-Johnston trans., Neptune Publications 2005) (*"Kyōhan* (Suzuki-Johnston trans.)"); *see also* Shōshin Nagamine, *Tales of Okinawa's Great Masters* (Patrick McCarthy trans., Tuttle 2000); Wikipedia contributors, *Sakugawa Kanga*, Wikipedia, *The Free Encyclopedia*, https://en.wikipedia.org/wiki/Sakugawa_Kanga

for an answer. To get rid of them, the Karate masters finally gave in and agreed (or so it seemed) to teach them the secret Kata. "This is Karate," they said. "Take it to your island but guard it with your life."

And so, Tōde-Sakugawa and others brought the secret knowledge back home, daily polishing the secret techniques. Then, they passed them down to others. "This is Karate," they said. No one asked questions – after all the techniques were "secret." The charade continued, spreading beyond tiny Okinawa to the whole of Japan, and now engulfing the world.

Of course, the Chinese teachers showed those "foreigners" only the outward encryptions of Kata techniques – divorced (without knowing the secret code) from what real Karate is about.[174] How could they do otherwise? Those were the deepest secrets belonging to their families and they were their sworn guardians.

Practicing Kata in Undecoded Form

If Kata do not show us their techniques directly, is there any redeeming value in performing them as passed down to us in the hidden encrypted form?

Of course there is. In their mission to encode Karate techniques in secret sets of motions, Kata creators gave full vent to their poetic license, creating true artistic masterpieces. In order to hide the true meaning, sometimes they left out an obvious part, sometimes they used a secret convention, sometimes they simplified elaborate movements totally beyond recognition of what lay behind. Obviously, we can benefit by rehearsing those masterpieces in their unrevealed form.

First, by performing Kata in their scripted forms, we circulate through our bodies the martial energies reposed in them. You may have noticed that after performing various Kata, the state of our body and mind changes, leaving us more or less invigorated. Indeed, the practice of Kata with the code uncracked resembles practicing Qigong forms for *Ki* transformation, purification and renewal – at least on the outside. To

---

[174] Much of what's missing in the encrypted form of Karate can be found in the the techniques of Aikido. This may become more evident by studying Kata applications in the back of this book.

fully benefit from such practice, we cannot move mindlessly without aim. We must engage our mind by visualizing the actual applications of techniques. This really gets the *Ki* moving. With each repetitively executed movement, we harness those energies, fortifying our martial spirit and refining *kime*.

Second, we practice Kata in their unrevealed form to remember what they contain.

Third, we practice Kata as handed down to us to honor their creators.

Do We Really Need Kata?

In Master Funakoshi's days, knowledge of Karate implied the ability to kill with one's bare knuckles. Practice was real, and punching techniques reached the level of perfection, their power lethal. Today, some still carry on the tradition, daily perfecting their punching techniques. But, unlike yesterday, today's punches, with their teleporting speed propelled by the power of turbocharged *Ki*, are virtually invisible to the eye and undetectable by the mind – truly beyond defense. Armed with such power, why do we still need Kata?

Only the uninitiated could ask such a question. As the old masters taught, Karate – with its ability to kill with one blow – carries an injunction not to use it, at least not in one-on-one personal encounters.

As I hope to demonstrate in the following chapters, Kata techniques are meant to fill in the space between becoming a victim of an attack and having to kill the aggressor. Kata represent the middle ground designed to stop a fight without having to use that fatal strike. Without the mediating assistance of Kata, the power of a Karate punch might be too much for most of us to control. Indeed, the biggest "secret" reposed in Kata is that Karate is not about fighting; it is about avoiding a fight. The secret seems impenetrable enough to remain a secret even after it is unequivocally disclosed.

The Do-Gooders

In Karate, we first learn basic stances and techniques, "learn" a few Kata sequences (in their encrypted form) and engage in pre-arranged *kumite*.

Although we progress in *kyū* (級) and *dan* (段) rankings, the meanings of most Kata movements continue to elude us.

A few of us will ask a question or two in an attempt to unlock Kata secrets and unite with the original intent of their creators. Our search, however, is often impeded; some well-intentioned practitioners, insisting that Kata be interpreted literally, exactly as handed down, have changed parts of the movements in their desire to improve them. Most of these improvements merely reflect their personal interpretations based on their own limited experience and knowledge. The dangers are obvious: the original intent and the accompanying spirit behind such altered movements may have forever been lost.

Some changes in Kata movements may have been innocuous. For example, introducing new stances, or substituting different ones does not particularly offend me. As I see it, *neko-ashi-dachi*, *kō-kutsu-dachi* and *fūdo-dachi* are closely related, judging from the position of the back leg, which is mostly the same. Consider, however, places where *yoko-geri-keage* replaced the traditional *mae-geri* when used in combination with *ura-ken-uchi* in several Kata. Does it make any sense? The original meaning of *mae-geri* becomes lost. The change merely obscures the original intent behind the movement.

Some have even concluded that certain Kata sequences appear to have been patched together for no particular reason. As Ohshima-sensei observed, "[i]nstructors have to make sure that each movement in the Kata conforms to Master Funakoshi's textbook and is executed exactly as the Master says. But, you'd be surprised, there are many incomplete parts in these Kata."[175]

Let's suspend our disbelief, however, and persevere in spite of the apparent roadblocks and obstacles. If we practice Kata with awareness, we may begin to discern patterns, similarities, and variations of the same technique. We may find the secret code to pierce through the shorthand notations and discover a new world where effective, combat-tested Karate techniques come to life.

Passing quick judgment on the perceived shortcomings of Kata techniques may in fact manifest our own shortcomings and inability to

---

[175] Ohshima-sensei, *Notes on Training* (cited in note 27) at 7.

penetrate deeper into their original intent. There is much more to Kata than meets the eye. By earnestly searching, we may turn the darkness of interpretational difficulties into the light of understanding, discovering the new meanings that have eluded us for so long.

Every Kata Has a Story

> *During the performance of Karate Kata, there were some people who were snickering because they felt that somehow they were watching a dance performance* (shimai), *but when the movements were explained through* kumite, *they were able to fully understand for the first time the meaning of Karate.*[176]

—Quoted by Master Funakoshi Gichin

On the surface, all Kata employ only a few basic techniques, such as blocks, kicks, and punches, which repeat themselves with minor variations. Looking closer, we may discern that many of these blocks and punches are in fact neither. Looking still deeper, we may notice that each Kata carries a theme of its own, not unlike a musical composition. Some Kata stress particular throwing techniques, others kicking or turning the opponent around. Some emphasize power, others emphasize agility.

Sometimes I think of Kata in terms of their salient techniques. My thinking may be colored by the throws I detect in their movements. For instance, over the years, I've been thinking of *Heian San-dan* as a story of the *gyaku-zuchi*[177],[178] and the *kubi-wa* throws, and of *Heian Go-dan* as a story of the *yari-tama* throw – three of the several throws described by Master Funakoshi in his written works.

Sometimes, the meaning of a Kata influences how I feel about it. Consider for example, the interplay of the two Chinese characters composing the name *"sōchin"* in *Sōchin* Kata (explained later in the book). From "vibrant tranquility or calm," to "tranquilizing manhood or

---

[176] Master Funakoshi, *Karate Jutsu* (cited in note 15) at 180-81, quoting from Tokyo Prefectural First Middle School publication (Gakuyūkai Zasshi), No. 86.

[177] The kanji of *gyaku-zuchi* (逆槌) allows for other readings, such as *saka-zuchi*.

[178] This throw was apparently misnamed as *tani-otoshi* in Master Funakoshi's *Karate Jutsu*; *see* Master Funakoshi, *Karate Jutsu* (cited in note 15) at 55.

strength" – can you resist the evoked imagery? In contrast, imagine the "flying swallow" in the name *Enpi* Kata – does it color your practice as you study the Kata's throwing techniques? Do you feel the energy of the big open sky above you when you contemplate or apply the techniques of *Kankū Dai*? I certainly do.

Challenge: *How many throwing techniques can you find in Enpi Kata?*

Hopefully, upon learning the meanings of Kata opening movements and analyzing them through the prism of applicable conventions, the themes within Kata will become more transparent and will allow you to create your own stories about them.

CHAPTER 8
The Why of Kata Opening Movements

When he was growing up, Master Funakoshi spent hours playing *tegumi* – a form of Okinawan wrestling of unknown origin – with other children. In fact, some people perceived a connection between *tegumi* and Karate. The very word *tegumi* is a reverse of *kumite*, deriving from *te*, meaning hand, and *kumu*, meaning joining, linking, crossing or grappling.

Although the young Funakoshi-sensei took *tegumi* practice most seriously, the rules were fairly benign: no use of fists to strike, no use of feet to kick, no *shu-tō-uchi* (knife-hand strike) and no *enpi-uchi* (elbow strike). As Master Funakoshi explained, "the bout begins, as sumō does, with the two opponents pushing against each other. Then, as it proceeds, grappling and throwing techniques are used."[179]

Could it be that those playful games of Okinawan children were just "warming-up" exercises for the more adult exercises of no-holds-barred Karate?

"Each Kata Begins with a Block" – Recognizing Nonsense

> *Our teachers did not give us a clear explanation of the Kata from old times. I must find the features and meaning of each form by my own study and effort, by repeating the exercises of form through training.*
> —Chitose Tsuyoshi-sensei

The often repeated phrase *Karate ni Sen-te Nashi* (there is no first hand (strike) in Karate) is emblematic of the art: No first strike in Karate. The opening movements of each Kata emphatically illustrate this point.

From the beginning, I was told that each Kata begins with *uke*, a block. The more I thought about it, however, the more I was beset by doubt. Take the opening movements of *Gankaku*, *Bassai Shō*, *Wankan*, or

---

[179] Master Funakoshi, *My Way of Life* (cited in note 14) at 122 – 124.

the two *Go-jū-shi-ho* Kata – it just didn't add up. Explanations from many teachers were simply unacceptable to me.

Or, for that matter, take *morote uke* – the opening move in *Kankū Shō* Kata – is it really a block, as I was repeatedly told? A block against an unusually powerful foe who cannot be stopped by a single-handed technique? Would you recommend using this block in *kumite* practice against a powerful partner? Would just applying more "force" against such a monstrous opponent really stop or deter them? I doubt it.

Few instructors have owned up to the mystery. Egami Shigeru-sensei, an accomplished student of Master Funakoshi, did have the courage to say that many of the opening *kamae* of the Kata mystified him.[180] Others, try as they would, managed to weave some elaborate, artificial-looking blocks into opening techniques.

Were my former teachers, and all *their* teachers wrong?

Kata Opening Movements as Means of Escape

Escaping a Fight: Karate 101

Each Kata begins with an escape from a grasping hold of the opponent. Yet, for ages, this simple message appears to have been lost on us. In fact, if you showed me a Kata that does not begin with an escaping technique (*hazushi-waza*), I would be suspicious of its authenticity.

In the *Methods of Practice* part of *Karate-Dō Kyōhan*, Master Funakoshi discusses the need to imagine and practice numerous escape techniques against attacks from the front, side or rear in a variety of forms, including defenses against "grasping a wrist, both wrists, the collar, hair, or hugging."[181] Indeed:

> The attacker may grasp the wrists, clothing, neck, or other
> parts of the body, and one must escape from his attempt to
> grasp and immediately deliver a counterattack. So the point

---

[180] Egami-sensei (cited in note 11) at 107 ("I know that there are changes in function among the various kata, but I must confess that I do not know the reason, nor why [kata ready stances] change according to the kata").

[181] *See* Master Funakoshi, *Kyōhan* (cited in note 6) at 235.

to remember is the quickness of the counterattack, which is executed almost simultaneously while escaping from the attacker's hold.[182]

To my astonishment, few if any have yet discerned that Kata opening moves are designed for practicing and analyzing ways to escape from such grasping attacks. How on earth has this fundamental aspect of Kata escaped our notice for so long?

Courage to Relax

The samurai who is always in a state of readiness is not simply one who, when he encounters any situation, grasps the situation and knows how to deal with it skillfully on the basis of his experience. Rather it is a matter of considering carefully the way one should handle all kinds of situations before they actually occur ….[183]

—Yamamoto Tsunetomo

Whether slow and forceful, or instantaneous, the application of power and speed in Kata opening moves demands that we control, receive and project *Ki*. The more we practice the more we can relax, regardless of what comes our way. As we relax, we empower *Ki* to flow freely, allowing us to quickly grasp what's happening around us and to react optimally. But if we do not relax, we restrict the flow of *Ki* and give an advantage to our opponent.

The ability to reach a state of complete relaxation regardless of perceived dangers is central to the mastery of Karate. Try to escape from a hold by using force and resistance. In doing so you'll meet with the even stronger force of your opponent. The stronger will invariably win. However, by fully relaxing, by making our hand limp, we can escape with relative ease. At first, when releasing hands from a grip, we may facilitate an escape by opening our hands widely just prior to a release. Later we will play naturally with the soft and hard energies within our hands. If we cannot do this, we cannot yet say we know Karate.

---

[182] *Ibid.*
[183] Yamamoto (cited in note 24) at 55.

Each Kata opening move teaches us to relax. Developing this state of softness, which can transform into the force of sudden *kime* – the harder aspect of Karate – is what we work on in our daily practice.

Tsukuri

> *If you want to attack east, first strike west.*[184]
>
> —Master Funakoshi Gichin

We spent hours experimenting with *kaki-wake* against holds to our *gi*, practicing as explained by seniors. Yet, our attempts to make this means of escape work were mostly in vain. Try as we might, the partner's hold seemed unbreakable. In the end, the exercises turned into a show of unrestrained pure strength – power against power. That is not Karate.

Add the concept of *tsukuri*, which is well developed in the world of judo, and new applications of techniques miraculously open up. The size and the strength of the opponent suddenly recede into the background!

In order to break a hold, we make the first movement in the direction opposite to where we intend to go – a concept known as *tsukuri*. Some of us may actually be performing *tsukuri* in our Kata opening moves without exactly knowing its meaning. For example, in *Kankū Shō's* first movement, we first draw the opponent to the right in order to more easily release their hold by applying *"morote uke."* This methodology is applicable to most methods of escape. Indeed, one precept on escaping, quoted by Master Funakoshi, tells us to first strike west if we want to attack east.[185]

Go east with the opponent if you intend to go west. Make them resist the initial eastward action to induce them to go westward with you. Try this with *kaki-wake*: the opponent who initiallly resists going east with you suddenly follows you all the way to the west. They're unwittingly sent sprawling on the floor! This is the power of *tsukuri*.

We should begin the opening movements of Kata with *tsukuri*, leading our partner away from where we want them to go. Their resistance will help us execute the first technique with relative ease. Interestingly,

---

[184] Master Funakoshi, *Karate Jutsu* (cited in note 15) at 176.

[185] *Ibid.*

a Kata's first movement is often our clue to understanding the meaning of its other techniques.

Is It Really Karate?

> *When there are no avenues of escape or one is caught even before any attempt to escape can be made, then for the first time the use of self-defense techniques should be considered.*[186]
>
> —Master Funakoshi Gichin

Taming Raw Strength

Some may object that interpreting opening Kata techniques as means of escape, while interesting, bears little relevance to Karate as *Budō*, not to mention Karate as a sport. On the contrary.

All too often, Karate students performing Kata (as encrypted movements), or engaging in sparring, move as if they were pieces of rigid machinery. Their techniques may look powerful, but they are not supple. Their reactions are slow. Their movements are impeded. They become easy victims to determined and nimble attackers.

They invariably use force to escape from a hold, provoking even more force from their aggressor. If the other person is stronger, there is virtually no chance of escape. Force against force! Is this what Karate is about?

Ideally, *Karate-ka* of whatever size should be able to overcome any opponent by using the opponent's physical strength to their own advantage. To do so, practitioners must know how to deploy soft and hard powers as the situation demands. Learning how to escape is meant to teach these skills.

We learn that escaping from a hold by positioning the opponent away from the escape route (*tsukuri*) and totally relaxing is easy, but by exerting strength is futile. This lesson can then be extended to other Karate techniques, and can prove invaluable in sparring with even stronger opponents. More important, cultivating a supple body will result in cultivating a supple mind.

---

[186] Master Funakoshi, *Kyōhan* (cited in note 6) at 234.

People Will Laugh at You

> *Practice diligently to avoid mistakes. A bystander viewing you may laugh, thinking your learning shallow [due to his lack of understanding]....*[187]
>
> —Master Funakoshi Gichin

Viewed from outside, our practice of Kata applications may look childish. Other students and even instructors may ridicule or laugh at us, especially if our interpretations are unfamiliar to them. That's OK. We don't follow The Way of *Budō* to please them, or to meekly conform to their expectations. Our mission is greater, and the responsibility to follow it is ours alone.

Playing with light and heavy applications of *Ki* may throw them for a loop. To those for whom Karate has only the hard side of outwardly powerful blocks and attacks, our notions may look immature and un-*Budō*-like. But their ignorance of the underlying principles of Karate should not stop us, or we will never progress.

Defending Against Strikes and Kicks

Knowing how to escape from holds and grabs directly translates to defending against strikes, kicks and other acts of violence. Imagine, if you will, that the aggressors' hands, which would have grabbed us, were actually trying to hit us. Think of "escaping" from such imaginary aggression **before** the aggressors' hands or kicks manage to reach our body. Suddenly, our familiar "means of escape" from static holds and grabs transform to blocks or deliveries of preemptive strikes in a dynamic set of motions.

The greater our ability to free ourselves from static holds, the greater our confidence when facing the direct threat of a moving attack. After learning to escape from holds, we can practice how to prevent the opponent from getting hold of us. We will learn to instinctively defend against all forms of violence and aggression.

---

[187] Master Funakoshi, *Karate Jutsu* (cited in note 15) at 175.

Practicing methods of escape also gives us opportunities to feel, identify with and seek unity with the opponent. We can then transfer this ability to *kumite*. More fundamentally, a good grounding in methods of escape may soften our edges in potential confrontations by cultivating a less combative demeanor. Instead of instinctively meeting force with force, our mental stance of restraint may turn potential aggressors around, leading to a peaceful resolution without a fight.

Finally, practicing *hazushi-waza* will make us better practitioners, equipping us with an arsenal of martial tools far beyond *tsuki-*, *keri-* or *uchi-waza*. What if our punch or strike fails? What if our kick misses? What if we just don't want to respond with a punch or a kick?

Escapes, Blocks or Attacks – Take Your Pick

As shown below in the Appendix (*Unlocking Kata Opening Movements*), I detected an application of *jū-ji-nage* in the characteristic movement of *Go-jū-shi-ho Shō* where, after the right open hand (手刀) moves gradually to the right, with the right elbow resting on the left wrist, both hands suddenly breaking away from each other in a snapping motion. Before I reached that understanding, however, I first imagined and applied this throwing technique as a defense not against a hold but against punches. I would block a right *jō-dan-zuki* and immediately get hold of the attacking hand with my right hand, and block a left punch and immediately seize the attacking hand with my left hand – it did not matter which punch came first. I would then follow up with *jū-ji nage*. However, to put the movement in sync with the original intent behind the Kata, I simply reverse-engineered the blocking/throwing sequence and recharacterized the entire movement as an escape from the opponent's hold.

The evolution of my understanding of the opening move of *Heian Ni-dan* further illustrates my early zeal to "accommodate" blocking and attacking techniques into what I now clearly see as Kata's means of escape. But even then, I knew better than to accept the left *"haiwan-uke"* of the Kata's first move as a block. In fact, I would urge my friends not to use it against *jō-dan* attacks – it would be simply too dangerous against powerful *furi-zuki*-like punches. Instead, I managed to reconfigure the first move of the Kata into a simultaneous *age-uke*-like block with my back hand[188] and a powerful strike with my front back fist (the Kata's *haiwan-uke*). For example, I would block my partner's left-hand punch with my left *age-uke* (or *haiwan-nagashi-uke*), shifting or guiding their striking arm backward, while striking *jō-dan* with my right *ura-ken*. The technique worked for me and I found it far safer and more effective than the application of the Kata's initial movement as officially taught.

The message: many escape techniques can be used against attacks other than holds or grabs. Once we know the principles of escape, we should be able to find alternate uses for them in many other combat situations.

The Why of Escape

> *We don't (even) carry small weapons.*
> (Mi ni suntetsu wo obizu.)
> *(身に寸鉄を帯びず)*

The methods of escape do not fit neatly into the contemporary concept of Karate. What the heck do "open hands," or the ways of escape have to do with it? Let's think again.

On a practical level, beginning each Kata with an escape reaffirms Karate's cardinal message of suppressing our urge to fight. But within the culture of retaliation and revenge – that condones dealing an opponent a powerful blow at the slightest provocation – this message rings hollow.

We are different. Rather than fighting, we seek to avoid using our lethal powers. Reacting with a powerful blow might be relatively easy but we don't do it. To do so would deal a blow to the spirit and dignity of *Budō*.

On a practical level, as followers of *Budō*, we don't care about getting hit or even saving our own lives. We are always ready to die for the right cause. Living in a world where "there are many despicable people who have no pride, who have no courage, who are full of avarice and think

---

[188] Perhaps more accurately, this block should be characterized as *haiwan-nagashi-uke*, or a back-arm sweeping block.

only of [themselves]," we should be "ready to throw away [our own lives]"[189] for a higher cause.

On a spiritual level, we escape from ourselves. Funakoshi-sensei has elevated the fighting techniques of tiny Okinawa to the glorious world of *Budō* simply by replacing the original Chinese character *"tō,"* or *"kara"* in Karate with a different character, also read *"kara"* but carrying the meaning of "empty."[190] Suddenly, with a stroke of the brush, "Karate" acquired its new identity: "empty hands."

By making this tiny change, Master Funakoshi imbued Karate with a spiritual dimension, calling on us to empty not just our hands, but our hearts and minds as well. Reaching beyond the mundane into the realm of spiritual "emptiness," the Master sent us in pursuit of freedom from spiritual limitations and personal attachments. This elevated state of spiritual liberation is often referred to in Buddhist philosophy as *gedatsu* (解脱).

The "opening" of Karate hands and hearts has further awesome spiritual implications for Karate's techniques of escape. More than simply escaping from an attacker's grasping hands, we escape from ourselves.

As used by Master Funakoshi, the Japanese word for "escape" (from opponents' physical holds) is also *"gedatsu,"* the same *gedatsu* used to mean escaping from our earthly bonds and written with the same Chinese characters. Whether dealing with spiritual bondage or physical aggressors, we practice Karate to free ourselves from them by mastering ways of escape. Isn't this inspiring?

---

[189] *See* Yamamoto (cited in note 24) at 50.

[190] When Master Funakoshi introduced Karate to the mainland of Japan, Karate was written as 唐手, pronounced either *"tō-de,"* or *"kara-te,"* where the character *"唐"* referred to the Tang dynasty, and people thought of Karate as "Chinese Hands."

CHAPTER 9
The Why of Other Kata Techniques

Demystifying Kata opening techniques opens the door for taking a fresh look at other Kata movements. Do they really – as currently taught – reflect Kata's original intent?

Surprise, Surprise – Recognizing Nonsense Continued

> I heard someone who professed to be an authority tell his astonished listeners that "in Karate we have a kata called nukite. Using only five fingers of one hand, a man may penetrate his adversary's rib cage, take hold of the bones, and tear them out of the body. …"
>
> "In Karate," they say, "a strong grip is essential. … The man who has strengthened his grip to the maximum … is easily capable of ripping the flesh of his adversary into strips."
>
> What nonsense![191]
>
> —Master Funakoshi Gichin

For years I dutifully applied the *tei-shō* "blocking" technique in *Jion* Kata against *chū-dan* attacks, complying with the official explanation that its purpose was to block an incoming hand or stick attack. I got pretty good at it. One time, my sparring partner suggested that this block looked somewhat risky and unsafe. At first I thought he was merely jealous that I could easily block his punches with this technique. On reflection, I studied this "block" further, eventually discovering its original intent. I am thankful to my partner – his innocent comment may have served as a catalyst for my discovery.

---

[191] Master Funakoshi, *My Way of Life* (cited at note 14) at 8 – 10 (from section entitled *Recognizing Nonsense*).

Similarly, for years I followed the conventional teaching that the rising punch (*jō-dan age-zuki*, or *furi-zuki* as it is sometimes referred to) in *Enpi* Kata was a punch directed to the chin. I kept experimenting. Training with partners with good straight posture, I found it challenging to reach their chins. Against more corpulent partners with prominent bellies, try as I would, it was impossible.

Then it hit me. Of course, the primary application of not only these two techniques but of most Kata techniques is to escape from hand holds, including techniques immediately following or performed in tandem with *hazushi-waza*, such as *nage-waza* (throwing techniques), *kansetsu-waza* (joint-locking techniques) or *shime-waza* (choking techniques).

Let's take a look at the "blocking" techniques of other Kata: *jū-ji-uke*, *morote-uke*, *shu-tō-uke*, or even *age-uke*. How often have you seen their application in sports Karate *kumite*? In fact, I find that for most people it is almost impossible to block a strong punch with a textbook form of *age-uke*, at least not without stepping out of the way with *tai-sabaki*. Now, compare the official explanations with the interpretation of these "blocks" as various means of escape from an attacker's grasping holds. Which makes more sense?

No more secrets. No more pretending. Techniques come to life. Awareness rises.

A "Punch" Is Not Always a "Punch"

Those for whom inflicting damage to the opponent is of paramount concern may never discover the original meaning and full beauty of our Kata. To them, punches will always be punches. Considering any other application is unacceptable, as it carries the potential of uprooting their notion of Karate as an elegant form of boxing.

Yet on deeper consideration techniques that look like punches or strikes begin to reveal other previously-unimagined applications, whether releases from handholds, or penetrations deep inside the opponent in preparation for a throw, a joint-locking technique, or a choke hold. Good examples of this are the "punches" in *Kankū Shō, Bassai Shō* or *Enpi* Kata, the "double punch" of *yama-zuki* in *Bassai Dai,* and the *ippon-ken* "punches" in *Hangetsu*.

Challenge: At first blush, the oi-zuki *of* Heian Sho-dan *look like lunge punches. But could they be used as a means of escape from the opponent's hold?*

Indeed, why would Kata creators clog their shorthand transcript of secret techniques with simple punches? Seems extravagant, a total waste. Or, are these punching techniques included there merely as protective decoys or deceptive ploys to throw nosy onlookers off?

Still, a Kata punch can always turn into a real punch, but this is the last resort. Once delivered, a real punch cannot be recalled. Before even considering anything of the sort, we strive to end any confrontation with the minimum aggression, giving the attacker a way out, a chance to reconsider. This is the message of Kata.

The Why of *Shu-Tō-Uke*

Karate should be practiced over and over so that the details of every movement are thoroughly grasped. You should practice them with a clear idea of how the techniques should be used in any situation.[192]

—Master Itosu Anko

Obviously not a traditional block. How often do we see its "blocking" application in a *kumite* tournament? Let's not kid ourselves. The technique is our system's beloved way of escaping from a two-hand hold.

It used to be done with *tsukuri* – by extending both hands toward the back – followed by a spectacular example of *jū-ji-nage*, an arms-crossed throw. Admittedly, to make this throw effective takes an enormous amount of practice – think about the countless hours Aikido practitioners spend perfecting their throws; not only to strengthen *Ki* channels for their techniques, but also to learn to fall without injury. *Ukemi san-nen*, a Japanese saying suggesting that it takes three years to learn how to break a fall, drives this point home.

The difficulty of a well-coordinated throw, however, can be alleviated by applying the *nuki-te* "attack" from *Heian Ni-Dan*. As you may suspect by now, this *nuki-te* is not meant for ripping into the opponent's ribcage with our three fingers. The open-hand *nuki-te* signifies grasping the opponent's

---

[192] Master Itosu Anko, quoted in Chitose-sensei (cited in note 10) at 112.

hand after crossing his arms with *"shu-tō-uke"* and pushing his hand by executing a subsequent *jū-ji-nage* technique.

Because of the difficulty of practical application and the danger of potential injuries, I believe that the form of *shu-tō-uke* was subsequently modified – eliminating the *tsukuri*. It continues however as *hazushi-waza* against a two-hand hold, with one hand grasping one of the opponent's hands while escaping with the other toward the back of our head in preparation for *shu-tō-uchi*.

Adding Dimensions to Kata: *Nage-Waza*

Master Funakoshi once said that Karate can be thought of as a "hard" form of martial arts with throwing techniques playing only a secondary role.[193] For many practitioners throwing techniques don't even play a tertiary role. Yet, they abound in our Kata.

Challenge: *How many throwing techniques can you find in your favorite Kata?*

We can relatively easily find applications of the throws introduced by Master Funakoshi in his *Karate Jutsu*. In the Appendix, I present a few of them while analyzing the meanings of Kata opening moves. There are many other takedown applications – the opening move of *Kankū Dai* for instance – with *jū-ji-nage* representing the favorite throw. Indeed, robbed of its throws, *Enpi* Kata would not only lose most of its luster and meaning, it would not exist.

I always experiment. Over the past few weeks, I was perfecting a variation of *kaiten-nage*. I like to perform it while applying a *tsuki-uke* against an upcoming punch by sliding my blocking hand under the opponent's elbow. Against a powerful partner, executing this throw may prove challenging. However, with practice, we find ways to make it relatively easy.

Challenge: *Can you find an application of* kaiten-nage *in our Kata?*

True, Karate is neither Judo nor Aikido. But why purposely cleanse its repertoire of techniques (*waza*) "belonging" to other martial arts? Why

---

[193] *See* Master Funakoshi, *Karate Jutsu* (cited in note 15) at 53.

limit ourselves? Someone just told me that for all his judo background, he finds that many applications of its techniques are impractical. I suggest that, unless practiced again and again, any *waza* may fail in an emergency. Let's broaden our vision in our relentless search for The Way.

Caution: *Because throwing techniques proliferate within Kata, the dangers of applying them cannot be overemphasized. As the previously quoted adage, "ukemi san-nen," suggests, learning falls (ukemi) is a mandatory condition of practice to reduce some of the accompanying dangers. Even experienced practitioners will sometimes sustain injuries while falling to the ground. A complementary study of Judo or Aikido falls would be a welcome addition to our practice with a view to opening up wider reaches of our Kata techniques.*

Shōrin-Ryū vs. *Shōrei-Ryū* Revisited

The recognition that Kata opening moves camouflage the application of escapes from holds and grabs by potential attackers elicits an interesting hypothesis: Could the fact that some escapes can be performed with relative ease, while others call for more force, confirm Master Funakoshi's thesis that *Shōrin-ryū* Kata favor people of lighter build whereas *Shōrei-ryū*[194] Kata better suit powerful people? I will let you decide.

Answer to Question from Section on Turbocharging and Triggering Release of *Ki* – The Why of *Hiki-te*: *By extending our heads up and feeling that they are suspended from above by a stream of Ki and by stretching the napes of our necks, we should be able to lower our arms even more.*

Which opening methods of escape can you perform with relative ease against strong opponents? Which opening moves are more difficult? Consider the fast opening moves of *Heian* Kata, *Enpi, Kankū Shō, Bassai* Kata, or *Gankaku* (typically classified as *Shōrin-ryū* Kata). Compare them with the first moves of the three *Tekki* Kata, *Jitte, Jion, Hangetsu* or *Sō-chin*

---

[194] Ohshima-sensei has clarified that *shōrei* name never existed and is a misspelling of *shokei*. In short, our classification concerns *shōrin* (also known as "Shaolin") and *shokei* styles. *See* Ohshima-sensei, *Notes on Training* (cited in note 27) at 53, 75.

(typically classified with *Shōrei-ryū* Kata). Can you perform them with equal ease?

Could Master Funakoshi have been right after all, despite some objections from his contemporaries?

As I see it, the controversy over which Kata belong to *Shōrin-ryū* and *Shōrei-ryū* stemmed from earlier *Karate-ka* ignorance of the meaning of Kata movements. Thus they could not explain why some Kata lend themselves to people with strong physiques while others suit people with slimmer and lighter bodies. Had they known what to look for, they would have abandoned their meaningless semantic squabble over the style name. Instead, they could have taken a fresh look and, by analyzing the methods of escape found in each Kata, reclassified them according to, for example, the ease and difficulty of applying those methods, or according to the main type of hold each Kata is designed to confront.

Kata Is One Thing, Actual Combat Another

> When practicing Karate, your eyes should glare with the feeling of actually going out onto the battlefield. … If you constantly practice this way, these skills will spontaneously appear on the battlefield.[195]
> —Master Itosu Anko

Our daily Kata practice purges our minds of inconsequential attachments. *Ki* flowing through our minds and bodies encodes our experience, little by little absorbing knowledge, constantly learning. *Ki* remembers. That's training. We believe that, when needed, techniques will manifest themselves exactly as we have rehearsed them with our partners.

Real combat, however, is unpredictable. There is less time to think how to apply techniques than we might wish. Adjusting to the demands of the situation may call for new applications of existing techniques, or discovery of new ones.

You may have already experienced that many techniques can be applied and interpreted in multiple ways. Can you think of additional variations? Holding on to a single pattern betrays a narrow mind unbecoming

---

[195] Master Itosu Anko, quoted in Chitose-sensei (cited in note 10) at 112.

a true martial artist and is incompatible with the spirit of real combat. A block can become a disabling attack. Every part of our body can serve as a weapon. A hold-escaping technique can suddenly become a rising punch or be combined with another attack, such as *enpi-uchi* (*hiji-ate*) or *tsuki-uke*. There are few tenets, few hard-and-fast rules in Karate. Form and formless constantly interchange.

Of course, many *hazushi-waza* can be used as actual blocks against oncoming strikes or kicks. In fact, this is the very essence of how Karate is practiced today. Such practice is essential – otherwise, we might find ourselves defenseless against direct striking attacks. But progressing from learning the means of escape to defending against violent attacks will make our reactions more reliable, adding an element of sharpness (*sae*) to our techniques and resulting in more powerful *kime*. More important, the ability to switch between light and heavy conditions of our hands, learned through practicing *hazushi-waza*, will make our blocks more effective and our strikes more lethal.

CHAPTER 10
The Why of the Kata Secret Code: Four Hidden Conventions

A student well versed in even one technique will naturally see corresponding points in other techniques. An upper level punch, a lower level punch, a front punch and a reverse punch are all essentially the same. Looking over thirty-odd Kata, he should be able to see that they are essentially variations on just a handful.[196]

—Master Funakoshi Gichin

Age-Old Mysteries Decoded

[Motobu Choki-sensei] was sad that with the popularity of [Karate] there also came great change too. The study of Kata in Tokyo had been carelessly changed, and in some cases completely disintegrated.[197]

—Nagamine Shōshin-sensei

Until recently, the mysteries of Kata have been sealed in a secret code. During the past 40 years I have uncovered and distilled several "major" conventions applicable to the entire system of our Kata – they are the keys to bring the hidden techniques into the open. I describe four of them below. Other, "minor" conventions find application in a few Kata only, and I describe some of them below in the Appendix.

The Open- and Closed-Hand Convention

I often wondered why the hands in Kata movements are sometimes open, sometimes clenched, sometimes forming *ippon-nuki-te*, sometimes *naka-daka-ippon-ken*, or sometimes *tei-shō*. I discovered that in most cases an open hand, in contrast to other hand forms, signifies seizing the

---

[196] Master Funakoshi, *Nyūmon* (cited in note 72) at 44.
[197] Nagamine Shōshin-sensei's reminiscences of Motobu Choki-sensei, as recounted in Motobu-sensei, *Watashi no Karate-jutsu* (cited in note 17) at 45.

opponent's hand. There may be exceptions (such as seizing the opponent's garments or other parts of the opponent's body) but this is the general rule.

I vaguely recall having executed the simultaneous double blocks (*ge-dan-barai* and *hira-kake-te*) in *Hangetsu* with an open hand. Then, at some point, the form of the hand changed to *ippon nuki-te*, as originally presented by Master Funakoshi. Note that *ippon nuki-te* is also used in *Unsu*, and *Go-jū-shi-ho Dai* (but not *Go-jū-shi-ho Shō*). For a long time I resisted my former teachers' explanations that *ippon nuki-te* in Kata are strikes to the body. Finally it struck me: the main purpose of this technique in Kata is to honor the convention, by telling the initiated that the double block (prior to the next technique) does not consist of swinging around the opponent's hands with our hands wrapped around them. The same is true in case of *ippon nuki-te* of *Unsu*.

Interestingly, to honor the convention, techniques involving the use of *tei-shō*, such as in *Jion*, *Enpi* or *Jitte*, are executed with fingers clenched at their second knuckles to leave little doubt that the hands of the opponent are not seized throughout the course of the movement.

The Opening-Movements Convention

I have already pointed out that each Kata opening movement represents a way of escape when our hands, arms or garments are grasped by the opponent. This rule has a universal application in all Kata. Each escape is then usually followed by an additional escaping technique, a throw, a joint-locking technique or a choking *waza*.

The Slow-Application-of-Power Convention

We don't need slowly executed moves in every Kata. In *Heian Sho-dan* or *Heian Ni-dan*, for example, all moves are executed quickly. In other Kata, rapid moves are interlaced with techniques, including opening moves, where power is applied gradually. For example, the first steps in *Jitte*, *Ni-jū-shi-ho*, *Sō-chin*, *Unsu*, *Kankū Dai*, *Hangetsu*, *Meikyō*, *Chin-te*, the two *Go-jū-shi-ho* and *Wankan* are performed slowly.

I've heard all sorts of explanations of the significance (or insignificance) of these slow moves. None carries much conviction. In particular, insisting that some Kata movements have little practical application strikes me as as a cop-out. Everything in Kata has meaning; the meaning is typically concealed, but nothing is redundant.

My best explanation is that these slow moves indicate escapes from holds grasping our garments – not holds against our wrists alone. Indeed, I find slowly-performed techniques to be excellent ways to escape from holds against our garments.

If all escapes were against holds grasping our hands, Kata applications would be too limited and divorced from more realistic scenarios where attackers might hold our arms, lapels or other parts of our clothes. They would resemble little more than the innocent games of children.

Nevertheless, each of our basic *Heian* (Peaceful) Kata begins with *hazushi-waza* against holds to our hands – apparently considered the least aggressive option. Is *Heian Yon-dan* an exception? I don't think so. As I understand it, its slow opening move used to be performed quickly until someone made the change, as discussed in the Appendix.

Interestingly, we can effectively apply some but not all slowly-performed techniques against holds directed to our hands alone. Such is the case, for example, with *kaki-wake* in various Kata, or the opening moves in *Kankū Dai*, *Chin-te* or *Unsu*. Other *waza*, such as the last moves of *Jion*, are designed mainly as releases from holds to our garments.

The *Embusen* Convention

Kata follow their own directions of movement, sometimes moving forward, backward, sideways or at an angle, always returning to the starting point. We call those patterns *embusen*. Yet, strictly holding on to the directions shown in the textbook while applying particular techniques serves absolutely no practical purpose.

Embusen is just a convention; it is not meant to be followed strictly. The real movements take on directions of their own, deviating from the prescribed route. For example, some techniques executed in a straight line are more effective following a circular movement. Other techniques need to adjust to the opponent's size and reactions. Still others need preparatory movements of *tsukuri*, which are often left to our imagination.

Other steps within Kata are mere simplifications or abbreviations of intended techniques. Even apart from the obvious need for secrecy, to convey complicated motions in a single Kata consisting of multiple techniques, their authors had to be creative, fixing the final forms as schematic portrayals of intended techniques.

In short, *embusen* is merely for reference, and rigidly sticking to prescribed courses of movement will prevent us from discovering the ultimate meanings of techniques.

Final Words – Rethinking Karate

Copying someone else's technique can, and will, never produce the same results as meticulous personal study and experience. Master the principles and the rest is easy.[198]

—Motobu Choki-sensei

Just by asking "why," we can demystify Karate and expose common errors and misdirected teaching methodologies. The following summarizes my research and findings for the improvement of our practice. This is by no means the final word.

First, we must ingrain in our hearts that the mission of Karate is to avoid unnecessary fighting. When analyzing Kata we should try to discover the least harmful interpretations of techniques, such as throws or means of escape. Remember that what looks like a punch is not always a punch.

Second, the practice of Karate should incorporate the awareness of Ying–and-Yang principles. When practicing Kata we should distinguish between light and heavy, and soft and hard application of *Ki*. Otherwise Kata practice is meaningless – instead of growing stronger we simply deplete our energies as time goes on, becoming weaker and weaker.

Third, we should practice moving our bodies by the power of *Ki* alone, cultivating and harnessing its energy with each repetition of a technique. Learning Kata's means of escape will help us effectively use *Ki* in harmony with changing circumstances. The risks of using muscular strength to power our techniques are grievous: premature depletion of vital energies and premature aging.

Fourth, Karate practice should aim at developing the most powerful *kime*. Without the power to kill we delude ourselves that we study Karate. To that end *maki-wara* training and the application of *ibuki*, *fumi-komi*, *me-sen* and synchronized focus of our energies are essential. For example, the commonly-seen overextension of the striking arm removes

---

[198] Motobu Choki-sensei, *Watashi no Karate-jutsu* (cited in note 17) at 16.

Karate from the land of *Budō* – the contraction of our body suffers, *kime* is compromised.

Fifth, the use of long stances as practiced today makes our *kime* less effective. Stances should become shorter and narrower to allow proper contraction of our lower back and inner thighs, and to allow sealing of the *ein* energy point to prevent unwanted leakage of *Ki*.

Sixth, it's time to rethink the role of *hiki-te*. As practiced today, the pulling hand twisted sideways loses connection not only with the potential target but also with our bodies – the contraction of our armpits and chest muscles becomes problematic. The role of *hiki-te* is not to twist our torso; it is to maintain a Yin-and-Yang balance of the striking unit of both hands as well as to pull our shoulders down to aid contraction of our body while squeezing our *tanden* to produce an extra impulse of *Ki*. It must be aligned in the direction of the potential target.

Seventh, it is time to ask "why" of even the most basic and generally accepted teaching concepts and theories behind techniques. Teachers who shy away from it belong to the world of yesterday. Today, both teachers and students should learn together. Awareness activates *Ki*. Mindful and meaningful application of techniques fills *Ki* with information. Without it our practice is self-defeating.

Finally, we must stop competing with others. It is a disgrace to the spirit of *Budō*, which with its power to kill should be contained and held sacred. We compete only with ourselves. Yes, we do compete – this is The Way.

Conclusion

To all those whose progress remains hampered by ego-related distractions, let humility – the spiritual cornerstone upon which Karate rests – serve to remind one to place virtue before vice, values before vanity and principles before personalities.

—Bushi Matsumura Sōkon

This book attempts to cover the immense territory of Karate, analyzing its fundamentals while offering a comprehensive and consistent framework for the interpretation of all Kata. If we choose to follow the principles outlined here, we must transcend our selfish desires (*gedatsu*) in our pursuit of The Way of ancient warriors. The quest will free us from the mundane. Let's use our growing powers to help and protect mankind. Let's never abuse them. Entry into this enchanted world will be its own reward.

By following The Way of *Budō* we can become better people. Yet, improving ourselves means nothing unless we share what we know with others and commit to improving the world we live in. Let's imitate Tseng Ts'an, who daily examined himself on three points: "Have I failed to be loyal in my work for others? Have I been false with my friends? Have I failed to pass on that which I was taught?"[199]

I will end with a quote from Master Funakoshi which I hope will resonate with you as it has with me over the years: "Make benevolence your lifelong duty. This surely is an important mission. It is a lifelong effort, truly a long journey."[200]

---

[199] Tseng Ts'an, quoted in *The Sayings of Confucius* 21 (James R. Ware trans., New American Library 1955).

[200] Master Funakoshi, *Kyōhan* (cited in note 6) at 248.

APPENDIX

Unlocking Kata Opening Movements

The steps within Kata movements illustrated below are referenced in parallel to (1) Sugiyama Shojiro-sensei's *25 Shōtō-kan Kata*, and (2) Nakayama Masatoshi-sensei's *Best Karate* series.

Points to Remember:

1. **The Importance of *Tsukuri*.** The effectiveness of a release from the opponent's hold usually depends on a coordinated application of *tsukuri* – usually by initially drawing the opponent where they resist to go: in the direction opposite to our intended movement.

2. **The Use of Leverage.** In addition to *tsukuri*, an effective release is often accomplished by applying leverage of our hands moving in opposite directions. Using one hand alone may prove ineffective against a powerful grip by a strong opponent. Sometimes even both our arms may not release their grip – additional leverage, such as twisting their thumbs – may be necessary.

3. **Deception within Kata.** Sometimes, Kata movements will not work by following the prescribed form. The actual intent may be hidden, concealed or simplified – it must be deduced after careful study. Sometimes the "right side" is the "left side;" sometimes the "back" is the "front;" and sometimes "up" is "down." The occasional snags are likely the unintended consequences of "improvements" by practitioners with shallow or incomplete understanding of the Kata.

4. **Remember the Purpose.** While practicing the application of these techniques, we should remember that our main purpose is to prevent an incident from escalating into a full-blown fight.

A simple release from the opponent's hold may often be enough. With that in mind, we'll be able to find the most effective ways to manifest the full potential of a technique. For each movement, think which hand you want to release and where you want the opponent to go.

5. **Deterrance First.** Sometimes to prevent a situation from escalating, a mere release from a hold may not be enough. To make the aggressor desist we may need to follow up with other techniques, such as throws, joint locks, chokes or even strikes to their vital points (*kyū-sho*), always remembering, however, that striking the opponent with a strong punch or causing injury should be our last resort.

Heian Sho-dan (平安初段)

Meaning: Peace/Calm – 1st of a Series

Other Name: *Pinan Sho-dan*

Former Name: *Pinan Ni-dan*

OpeningMovement–Opponent Holds Both Our Hands (Steps 1-2): The first movement could be a release from a two-hand hold by the opponent. In Kata, before the left hand sweeps the hand holding our right hand, we raise it toward our right shoulder. The function of this is first to release our left hand from the opponent's grasp. To help release our left hand from the grip of a strong opponent, we first place our right hand (which is still held by the opponent's other hand) over the opponent's right hand – which will add leverage to facilitate the release – and then pull our left hand up. Once we have

released our right hand from the opponent's grip by a downward sweep of our left arm, we have many possibilities of action. For example, we could seize his left hand and lead him toward the left in another preparatory action (*tsukuri*). Then, reversing direction, we could swing our left arm upward against his neck, throwing him down with a throw called *irimi-nage*.

121

Vignettes from Heian Sho-dan

25 SHŌTŌ-KAN KATA: **STEPS 7-9** (*Age-uke*)
BEST KARATE: **STEPS 7-9** (*Age-uke*)

There are many possible applications of *age-uke*.

1. We could use *age-uke* to free our hand held by the opponent. We could then grab the opponent's hand and pull it to the side in order to unbalance him.

2. Alternately, we can quickly change hands by grasping the opponent's hand with our other hand which reaches the opponent's hand by performing a second *age-uke*.

3. When both our hands are grabbed we could also escape, say with our right hand, by shifting our left hand under the opponent's left hand (crossing our forearms) to help escape with our right hand (we might also grab the opponent's left hand with our left hand). Then, we could cross our forearms again to escape with our left hand.

4. Needless to say, *age-uke* could serve us as a defensive weapon of attack. For example, we could strike the opponent with the forearm of our rising arm, aiming at his throat while pulling him towards us with our other hand.

5. Application with *kokyū-nage* (refer to the photos below): While being held by both hands, we perform *age-uke* with our left hand, releasing our right hand. Simultaneously we grasp his left hand with our left hand which just performed *age-uke*. We continue with right *age-uke* under the opponent's chin, extend our right hand along his neck and throw him down by pressing with our right arm and pulling his left hand with our left. *De-ashi-barai* or some other leg-sweeping technique with our right leg should make this throw more effective.

Heian Ni-dan (平安二段 *or* 平安弐段)

Meaning: Peace/Calm – 2nd of a Series

Other Name: *Pinan Ni-dan*

Former Name: *Pinan Sho-dan*

Opening Movement – Opponent Holds Both Our Hands (Steps 1 through 3): The first movement could be an escape from a two-hand hold by the opponent. First we pull him, by *tsukuri*, toward the back of our right side with our left hand underneath his left hand. Then we reverse the movement, with the left hand releasing our right hand, ending in the final position of Step 1 of the Kata. Although this movement will normally release both hands and no further escaping action is necessary, we follow up by grasping his left hand with our left and wrapping our right arm around his neck from behind. Turning our right arm upward against his chin we throw him down in a circular motion to the right (with a variation of a *kubi-wa* throw).

Vignettes from Heian Ni-dan

25 SHŌTŌ-KAN KATA: **STEPS 10-11** (*Shu-tō-uke* plus *nuki-te*)

BEST KARATE: **STEPS 9-11** (*Shu-tō-uke* plus *nuki-te*)

Opponent Holds Both Our Hands.

STEP 10: We pivot to the right (*tsukuri* to our right), grasping the opponent's left hand with our left hand at the wrist (our left hand will initially go over their right hand) and their right hand also at the wrist with our right hand. Then we reverse the motion of our hands, now moving forward into *jū-ji-nage* by pushing his bent right arm against his left elbow toward his shoulder.

STEP 11: We continue the throw by continuing with our right hand, which holds the opponent's right hand. In other words, the *"nuki-te"* aspect connotes holding the opponent's hand.

(The photographs below show a mirror image of these movements.)

Heian San-dan (平安三段 *or* 平安参段)

Meaning: Peace/Calm – 3rd of a Series

Former/Other Name: *Pinan San-dan*

Opening Movement – Opponent Holds Both Our Hands (Steps 1 through 3): First we pull the opponent by *tsukuri* toward the back of our right side, then we reverse direction and, by executing *uchi-uke*, release both our hands. In a follow-up action we embrace the opponent with our right arm going across his front torso and our left arm going toward his back in preparation for a *gyaku-zuchi* throw (one of the throws demonstrated by Master Funakoshi in his *Karate-Do Kyōhan*). As this throw may present a challenge against a heavy opponent, an *aiki-otoshi* drop from the Aikido repertoire might offer a more effective solution. In this throw, we squeeze the opponent's knees and throw them in an upward motion away from us

with our knee behind him facilitating the drop. Alternatively, we could apply a scooping throw – *sukui-nage*.

129

Vignettes from Heian San-dan

25 SHŌTŌ-KAN KATA: **STEPS 18-20**
BEST KARATE: **STEPS 18-20**

Opponent Holds Both Our Hands. We release our left hand by grasping his right hand with our right (which may still be held by his left hand) and pushing it away to the right. Doing so, we find ourselves behind him. We then grab him from the back with our left hand while sliding our right arm around his neck in preparation for a *kubi-wa* throw.

Heian Yon-dan (平安四段)

Meaning: Peace/Calm – 4th of a Series

Former/Other Name: *Pinan Yon-dan*

Opening Movement – Opponent Holds Both Our Hands: As practiced today, *Heian Yon-dan* opens up fairly slowly, indicating a release from a garment hold. As Ohshima Tsutomu-sensei points out, however, according to people who practiced with Funakoshi-sensei before the 1940s, this opening move was performed with normal speed, not unlike the opening movement of *Heian Ni-dan*.[201] This would indicate that its original intent was likely a release from a wrist grab. The technique works in either case.

Against a two-hand hold by the opponent, we pivot to the right (*tsukuri* to our right to create resistance) while grasping his left hand with our left and his right hand with our right. Reversing direction, we swing his left arm over his head turning his body around, his back facing us, leaving his shoulders in a vulnerable condition. A number of arm-locking techniques could also be applied in this situation. (The photographs below show a mirror image of these movements.)

---

[201] *See* Ohshima-sensei, *Notes on Practice* (cited in note 27) at 22.

Vignettes from Heian Yon-dan

25 SHŌTŌ-KAN KATA: **STEPS 5-6**
BEST KARATE: **STEPS 5-7**

Opponent Holds Both Our Hands. We draw the opponent deep toward our right side (*tsukuri* to our right), inducing him to step in with his left leg – opening himself to *mae-geri* with our left leg as a result. Simultaneously, we slide our left fist under his left arm. Reversing direction we swing our left back fist (*ura-ken*) to the left to release our right arm while executing a front kick with our left leg.[202] We follow up the movement by applying *hiji-ate* (elbow strike) or *ude-gatame* to his left elbow (refer to photo of *ude-gatame* in the opening movement of *Tekki Sho-dan*).

Challenge: If our objective is to draw the opponent's left leg in the direction of our initial pull, what could be the significance of bringing our left foot toward our right knee? Can you find similar movements in other Kata?

Challenge: Can you visualize the application of these movements without looking at photographs? Can you recognize the unified meaning of enpi strike against a forearm (mae-enpi) in the various Kata?

25 SHŌTŌ-KAN KATA: **STEPS 9-11**
BEST KARATE: **STEPS 11-13**

Challenge: Bearing in mind the opening movement of this Kata, how do you interpret the first two moves? Is the last step in the series a continuation of those movements or a separate technique? Can you find similar movements in Kankū Dai?

---

[202] The kick is directed toward the opponent's crotch. In this context, let's note Master Funakoshi's admonition on the subject:

> When caught off guard and it becomes absolutely necessary to do so, or when both of one's hands are jammed or grabbed by the opponent, one has no choice but to kick his testicles. This technique is called *kinteki*, but it should only be used in cases of life or death.

Master Funakoshi, *Karate Jutsu* (cited in note 15) at 51.

Heian Go-dan (平安五段)

Meaning: Peace/Calm – 5th of a Series

Former/Other Name: *Pinan Go-dan*

Opening Movement – Opponent Holds Both Our Hands (Steps 1 through 3): After pulling the opponent to the right (by *tsukuri*) and releasing our left hand, we release our right hand from the opponent's grasp by applying *uchi-uke* with our left hand. Then we immediately slide our left hand into the opponent's crotch while grabbing them from above in preparation for a *kata-wa-guruma*-type throw.

Vignettes from Heian Go-dan

25 SHŌTŌ-KAN KATA: STEP 9-10 (10A, 10B & 10C)
BEST KARATE: STEPS 9-10

Opponent Holds Both Our Hands. We cross our arms while lifting them up, releasing our left hand. This movement also acts as *tsukuri* for the subsequent application of an elbow/arm lock such as *neji-daoshi* (as shown by Master Funakoshi in his *Karate Jutsu*)[203] or *ude-gatame*.

---

[203] Note that that technique was labeled as *koma-nage* in Master Funakoshi's *Kyōhan*.

Tekki Sho-dan (鉄騎初段)

Meaning: (Riding) an Iron Horse – 1st of a Series

Former/Other Name: *Naihanchi Sho-dan*

Opening Movement – Opponent Holds Both Our Hands (Steps 1 through 3): When pulling the opponent to the left side by *tsukuri*, we simultaneously grasp his right hand with our right and his left with our left. Reversing motion, we turn the opponent around in a large circular motion of our right hand to make his back face us, continuously holding on to his right hand. If necessary, we step over his protruding right leg by raising our right leg. Continuing to the next move (*mae-enpi*), we may attack his right elbow with techniques such as *ude-gatame* or *enpi-uchi* (*hiji-ate*).

Challenge: Do you think that the applications of mae-enpi *in other Kata could be the same as those in* Tekki Sho-dan? *If so, you have unearthed yet another minor Kata convention.*

Vignettes from Tekki Sho-dan

25 SHŌTŌ-KAN KATA: **STEPS 34-35**
BEST KARATE: **STEPS 28-29**

Opponent Holds Both Our Hands. In preparation for a release (*tsukuri*), we move – in a circular motion to the left – our right hand over the opponent's left arm and our left hand over his right hand (our fists move counter-clockwise over his hands). Then we reverse direction while continuing the circular motion of our arms, swinging them to the right and up, accomplishing release of both our hands.

Bassai Dai (抜塞大)

Traditional Meaning: Seizing/Penetrating/Destroying a Fortress – Major/Big

Former/Other Name: *Passai Dai*

Taking Another Look: The foregoing translation nicely fits the concept of Karate as a fighting art designed to crush and destroy the enemy. But what about *Būdo's* cardinal teaching of avoiding fighting? What about the primary design of Kata techniques to allow us first to slip out from the opponent's hold while inflicting a limited and measured amount of damage, and only then, if all else fails, end with a mortal strike? Looking at the name of the Kata in this spirit, new translations of *Bassai Dai*, with less belligerent overtones, begin to emerge.

First Kanji of Bassai: The first kanji of *Bassai* is read *batsu* (*on-yomi*) or *nuku* (*kun-yomi*), and indicates a notion of "slipping out," "extracting," or "pulling out." The second character, *sai*, means "fortress." The last character, *dai*, means "big." Therefore, a more appropriate translation of the name could be something like "slipping out of a big fortress." If the author of the Kata wanted to convey the meaning of "piercing" or "destruction" in its name, they could have easily done so by using the kanji used in *nuki-te*.[204]

---

[204] The kanji used in *nuki-te* (貫) is used to write the Japanese verb *tsuranuku* (貫く), which indeed means to pierce, go through or penetrate.

Which imagery resonates with you when you study the movements and applications of this Kata?

Second Kanji of Bassai: The second kanji of *Bassai* is *sai* or *soku* (*on-yomi* readings) also pronounced *fusa(gu), toride* or *mi(chiru)* (*kun-yomi* readings). It carries the meanings of closure, obstruction, shutting or blocking. In combination with another character, *sai* can indeed signify a fortress, as in *yōsai* (要塞) and I agree with this interpretation.

Meaning of *Dai*: *Dai* (大) means big, large.

Suggested Revised Meaning: Slipping Out of a Big Fortress

Opening Movement:

Simple Release – Opponent Holds Both Our Hands: In preparation for a release (*tsukuri*), we pull the opponent to the left, sliding our right hand over his left and underneath his right hand while grasping his left hand with our left. Then by reversing our movement and shifting to the right, we press on his right arm with our right forearm, pushing his left hand with our left. This should release our hands and might even throw the opponent to the ground.

Thematically Integrated Version – Opponent Holds Our Garments:
Following *tsukuri* to our left, we induce the opponent to make a step with
his right leg. We then slide our right hand underneath his right leg in a
scooping motion, reverse direction of our motion, and with a circular
upward movement of our right hand we lift his leg to throw him down.

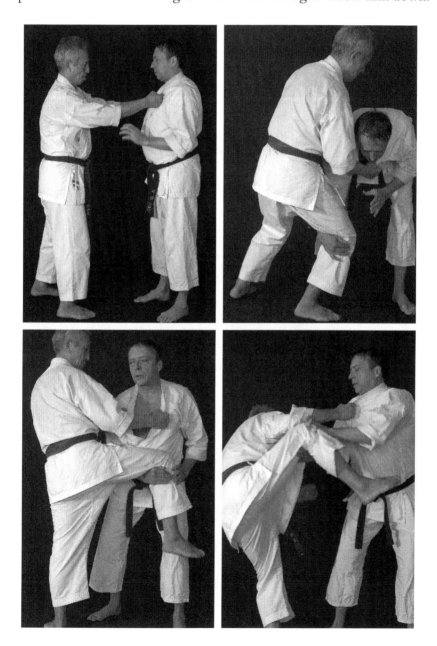

Vignettes from Bassai Dai

25 SHŌTŌ-KAN KATA: STEP 40

BEST KARATE: STEPS 38-39

Opponent Holds Both Our Hands. In preparation for a release (*tsukuri*), we swing our right arm underneath his arms to the left, and, again reversing our motion, we press our right forearm against his right arm, effecting release of both our hands.

(Digression: As taught in some *dōjō*, the swing of our right arm toward the left deflects an opponent's right front kick, and then, as our arm continues in a circular motion, sends his leg to our right with his back toward us. Although most people cannot perform such a block, it does not mean it cannot be done.)

25 SHŌTŌ-KAN KATA: **STEPS 35-39** (*yama-zuki*)
BEST KARATE: **STEPS 32-37**

Opponent Holds Both Our Hands. This could be an application of a *sukui-nage, katawa-guruma,* or even *kata-guruma.*

Application of *katawa-guruma* and *kata-guruma*
In *katawa-guruma*, we first perform *tsukuri* to our left releasing our right hand and inducing the opponent to step in with his right leg forward, then we slip our left hand inside his crotch and throw him down by lifting his leg while pulling his collar down with the other hand. In *kata-guruma*, we get deeper inside the opponent with our head placed outside his body from underneath him.

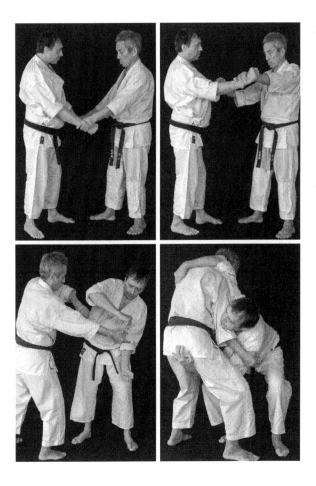

Kankū Dai (観空大)

Former Names: *Kūsankū, Kō-shō-kun* (公相君), *Kwanku*

Meaning: Looking at the Sky – Big/Major

Proposed New Meaning: Looking at the Big Sky

Opening Movement – Opponent Holds Our Garments: Performing *tsukuri* to our left, we swing our right arm over his left arm, and, after getting hold of his right hand with both our hands, wrench its hold away from our garments. If tearing his grip from our garments proves challenging, catching hold of his thumb should do the trick. Reversing direction, we raise his right arm, release his right-hand grip from our garments, and twist him around. Then, our right hand "feeds" his right hand to our left hand – this is the meaning of our right *shu-tō* connecting with the palm (*hira*) of our left hand in the beginning movement of the Kata. Continuing the movement of his right arm – this time with our left hand – we now raise his right arm up while keeping his head down with our right hand in preparation for a *kaiten-nage* throw.

Opening Movement – Opponent Holds Both Our Hands: We swing our arms upward while grasping his left hand with our right. We continue the motion of our right hand in a circular path downward, twisting the opponent around in order to seize his right hand with our left and release our right hand. We then pull on the opponent's right shoulder with our right hand, pushing his left hand upward with our left hand, bringing him to the ground.

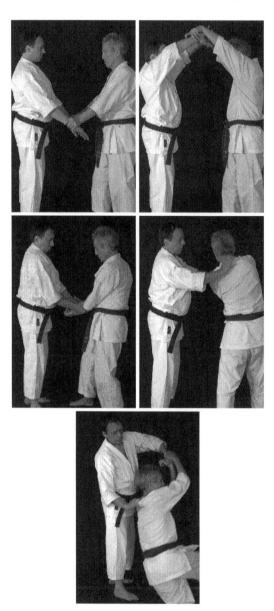

Vignettes from Kankū Dai

25 SHŌTŌ-KAN KATA: **STEPS 4-8**
BEST KARATE: **STEPS 5-7**

Opponent Holds Our Garments: We slide our left arm underneath his left arm while performing *tsukuri* to our right. Reversing our motion, we release his left-hand grip and, with our left hand, guide his left arm to the left in order to turn him away from us. We then quickly move around him and with our right arm encircle his neck, apply a variety of chokes, such as *hadaka-jime*, or take him down with a variation of a *kubi-wa* throw.

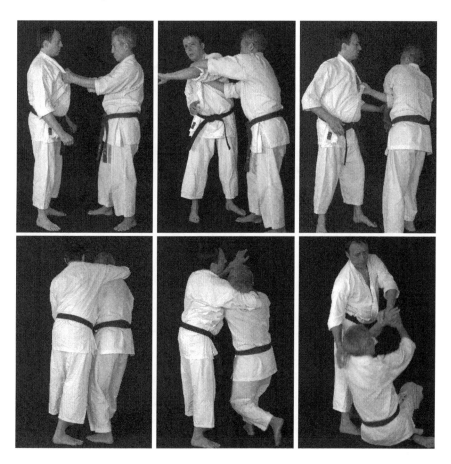

Opponent Holds Both Our Hands: The sequence of movements is almost the same.

Jion (慈恩)

Meaning: Both kanji evoke concepts relating to mercy, grace and kindness.

Name Derivation: Probably named after a temple.

Opening Movement – Opponent Holds Both Our Hands: We perform *tsukuri* to our left, followed by "blocking" his right arm with our right *uchi-uke* while pulling our left hand to our left hip, which releases our left hand. The subsequent *kaki-wake* will help us release our right hand. *Kaki-wake-uke* can also be performed independently to release ourselves from a garment hold, as shown in the opening movement of *Wankan*.

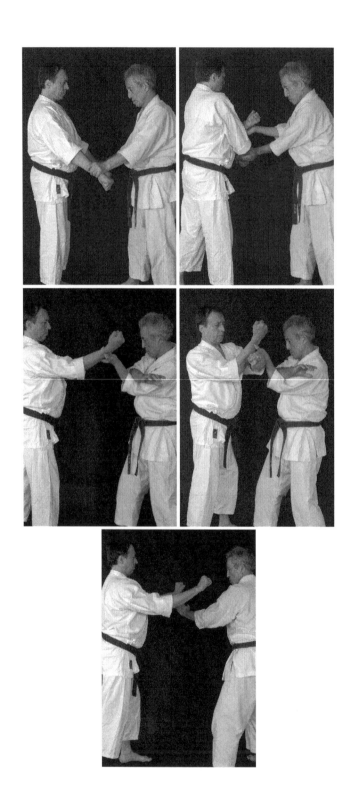

Vignettes from Jion

25 SHŌTŌ-KAN KATA: **STEPS 34-37**

BEST KARATE: **STEPS 34-37**

Opponent Holds Both Our Hands: As soon as we have applied *jō-dan jū-ji-uke* with our right hand in front of our left, we push his right arm (from which we just released our left hand) with our right hand, and, assisted by our left hand, turn the opponent so that his back faces us. We quickly slide our left forearm underneath his chin, placing our left palm on our right bicep and, bringing our head close to his, apply a variation of the *hadaka-jime* choking technique.

Enpi (燕飛)

Meaning: Flying Swallow

Former/Other Name: *Wanshū* (ワンシュウ)

Opening Movement – Opponent Holds Both Our Hands (Steps 1 through 2): In this release, we bring our right hand to our left while grasping the opponent's left hand with our left. As we feed his left hand to our left hand (the meaning of the initial *kamae*), we simultaneously release our right hand from his grip. Holding onto his left hand, we kneel down scooping his right leg with our right hand from outside. Standing up, we throw the opponent down with a *sukui-nage* type of throw. A strong *tsukuri* which induces the

opponent to step forward with his right leg is important to the success of this leg-scooping throw. Leg grabbing takedowns are referred to as *kata-ashi-dori* in Japanese, and can be performed by grabbing the opponent's leg either from the outside or from the inside.

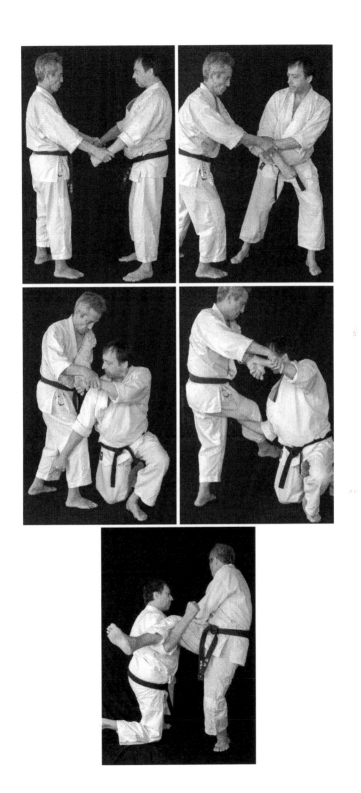

Vignettes from Enpi

25 SHŌTŌ-KAN KATA: STEPS 5-8 & 9-12 &25-28
BEST KARATE: STEPS 5-8 & 9-12 & 25-28

Opponent Holds Both Our Hands: We first release our right hand – this could be the application of the *ge-dan-barai*-like motion. With our freed hand we strike his right arm with a right *"age-zuki,"* releasing our left hand and simultaneously grasping his right hand with our right.

FOLLOW-UP ACTION:

Thematically consistent variation: Turning around to the left, we scoop his left leg around the knee with our left hand, and, as in the opening movement, we throw the opponent down by lifting his leg up.

Other variations: Giving free play to our imagination, after releasing our left hand with the *age-zuki*-like strike, we could apply a number of techniques. For example, grabbing his left hand with our left hand we position his hands into a *jū-ji-nage* initial position, and, twisting our body clockwise, extend our left leg in preparation for a throwing technique such as *tai-otoshi*. Or, we could just apply a joint lock to the elbow of the hand which we just release with our *"age-zuki."* Or, we could wrap our right arm around his neck and apply a *kubi-wa* throw.

Hangetsu (半月)

Meaning: Half Moon

Former/Other Name: *Seishan* (セーシャン)

Opening Movement – Opponent Holds Our Garments (Steps 1 through 3): First we perform *tsukuri* to our right, then we redirect the momentum to the left against the opponent's left hand with left *uchi-uke* – releasing his left-hand hold. Finally we slide our right arm underneath his right and strike his left arm with right *uchi-uke* – releasing his right-hand hold. The same sequence of movements can be performed against a two-hand hold of our hands. Alternatively, after the first *uchi-uke*, we simply push him away with both arms.

Vignettes from Hangetsu

25 SHŌTŌ-KAN KATA:	**STEPS 7A, 7B & 8A**
BEST KARATE:	**STEPS 6-8**

Opponent Holds Our Garments: We grasp the opponent's lapels with our hands: right lapel with left hand and left lapel with right hand, applying a *ryō-te jime* choking technique. Alternatively, we may slide our right hand toward his neck, getting hold of his right lapel, while grasping his left lapel with our left hand moving under our right. Pulling our hands toward us, we perform a *jū-ji-jime* choking technique. We can grasp his lapels with palms facing down for *nami-jū-ji-jime* or palms facing up for *gyaku-jū-ji-jime.* Finally, having accomplished the release, we push the opponent forward by extending our arms.

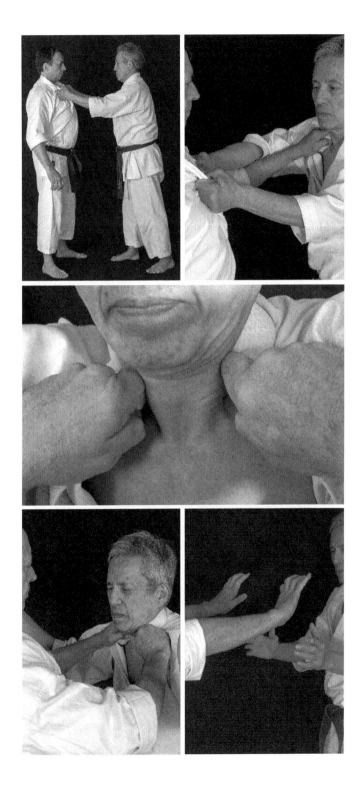

Jitte (十手)

Meaning: Ten Hands

Opening Movement – Opponent Holds Our Garments (Steps 1 through 3): Performing *tsukuri* to our left, after moving our right arm over the opponent's left arm, we insert our right arm underneath his right arm, while placing our left hand over his left arm. Reversing direction, we secure our hold of his left hand with our left, and his right hand with our right in preparation for *jū-ji-nage* to the right.

163

Opening Movement – Opponent Holds Both Our Hands (Steps 1 through 3): Performing *tsukuri* to our left, we slide our right arm over his left and underneath his right arm, simultaneously grasping his right hand with our left. Reversing direction and grabbing his right hand with our right, we perform *jū-ji-nage*.

Vignettes from Jitte

25 SHŌTŌ-KAN KATA: **STEPS 4-6**
BEST KARATE: **STEPS 5-7**

Opponent Holds Both Our Hands: To release our hands, we press with our *tei-shō* against his wrists in a snapping motion. This is the same application of *tei-shō* as in *Jion.*

Gankaku (岩鶴)

Meaning: Crane on a Rock

Former/Other Name: *Chintō* (チントウ)

Opening Movement – Opponent Holds Both Our Hands: This could be an application of a throwing technique using an *ude-garami* arm lock. First we perform *tsukuri* to our right, then we position our hands for *ude-garami* – our left hand holding on to his right hand and our right hand grasping our own left hand from underneath his right hand – and with a circular motion of our hands, throw the opponent down.

Vignettes from Gankaku

25 SHŌTŌ-KAN KATA: **STEPS 21-23**
BEST KARATE: **STEPS 21-24**

Opponent Holds Both Our Hands: Applying *tsukuri*, we pull the opponent to the right with our fists touching our waist and elbows extended sideways. Reversing direction, we swing our right elbow underneath his right arm, releasing our right hand. We refer to this motion as *hiji-uke*. Reversing our motion again, we press our right forearm against his right arm with *hiraki-uke* to effect release of our left hand. (You may recall that a release of our left hand following a *hiji-uke* with our right elbow in *Heian San-dan* was accomplished by a circular motion of our right arm in an *uraken-uchi*-like vertical strike.)

As we practice the release with *hiji-uke*, we may also find that by directing this block toward the opposite arm of the opponent (swinging our right elbow toward the right elbow of the opponent), we may often accomplish release of both our hands without the need for further *hazushi-waza*.

Tekki Ni-dan (鉄騎二段)

Meaning: (Riding) an Iron Horse – 2nd of a Series

Former/Other Name: *Naihanchi Ni-dan*

Opening Movement – Opponent Holds Both Our Hands (Steps 1-2): Performing *tsukuri* to our left, we lift our hands close to each other just like in the Kata, with our hands moving outside his right arm. Reversing our movement, we press against his hands, releasing his grip. If his leg stands in the way, we lift our right leg to avoid it.

In a more orthodox application, we could escape from the opponent's bear hug from the back by sinking down and lifting our elbows. While doing so, we could grab one of his hands and, after escaping his hold, apply an armlock to his elbow.

Opening Movement – Opponent Holds Our Garments: In this situation, our escape would resemble the application of *kaki-wake* (see *Wankan*, below).

Vignettes from Tekki Ni-dan

25 SHŌTŌ-KAN KATA: **STEP 11**
BEST KARATE: **STEPS 11a & 11b**

Opponent Holds Both Our Hands: Performing *tsukuri* to our right, we catch his left hand with our left. Reversing our motion, we apply an arm-lock to his elbow, pressing with our elbow (*ude-gatame*) while holding on to his wrist. While performing this *kansetsu-waza*, we continue looking at the opponent.

Tekki San-dan (鉄騎三段)

Meaning: (Riding) an Iron Horse – 3rd of a Series

Former/Other Name: *Naihanchi San-dan*

Opening Movement – Opponent Holds Both Our Hands (Steps 1-2): While performing *tsukuri* to our right, we swing our left hand to the right underneath our right hand, and, reversing the motion, we release our right hand by applying *uchi-uke* with our left hand. If the opponent continues holding our left hand, we reverse our motion again and release our left hand by executing *uchi-uke* against his right arm.

Vignettes from Tekki San-dan

25 SHŌTŌ-KAN KATA: **STEPS 6-8 & 22-24**
BEST KARATE: **STEPS 6-8 & 23-25**

Opponent Holds Both Our Hands: First, we catch his left wrist with our left hand while freeing our right arm by pulling it away from his grip. Then, we quickly pivot counter-clockwise and apply *hiji-shime* to his left elbow.

Ni-jū-shi-ho (二十四歩)

Meaning: Twenty-Four Steps

Opening Movement – Opponent Holds Both Our Hands (Steps 1 through 4): Moving back, we grasp the opponent's left hand with our left hand while freeing our right hand by pulling it to our side. Moving forward, we slide our right hand under his right hand which is still holding on to our left hand. After grasping his right hand with our right hand, we pivot clockwise, swinging the opponent's arms in a wide circle and turning him around so that his back is facing us. Our resulting hold of his arms leaves him with his shoulders in a vulnerable position.

Vignettes from Ni-jū-shi-ho

25 SHŌTŌ-KAN KATA: **STEPS 16-18**
BEST KARATE: **STEPS 16-18**

Opponent Holds Both Our Hands: We slide our right hand under his right hand while performing *tsukuri* to our left. Reversing motion, we release our left hand with a *maki-otoshi-uke* movement of our right hand and simultaneously get hold of his right hand. We then cross over with our left hand from above, grasping his left hand with our left. Reversing our motion again, with a wide swing of our hands, we move his hands in a circular motion, ending with his right hand up and left hand down. The next step (swinging our left hand up) is designed to inflict damage to his shoulders. (The photographs below show a variation of the movements.)

Chin-te (珍手)

Meaning: Strange/Curious Hands

Opening Movement – Opponent Holds Both Our Hands: We first free our right hand by using leverage of getting hold of the opponent's left forearm with our left hand. Then, while performing *tsukuri* to our left, we slide our right arm underneath his right hand. Reversing our motion, we continue swinging our right arm in a circular motion to release our left hand from his grip.

The photographs below show an escape when the opponent holds our garments.

Vignettes from Chin-te

25 SHŌTŌ-KAN KATA: **STEPS 27-28**
BEST KARATE: **STEPS 27-28**

Opponent Holds Both Our Hands: We attack the opponent with our head while swinging both our arms toward the back to secure their release (the swinging of our arms alone is not likely to release his grip). With our hands free, we immediately take him down by applying an *ude-wa* throw (one of the throws demonstrated by Master Funakoshi in his written works). A hip throw such as *koshi-nage* or *ō-goshi* would also work well in this situation.

Sō-chin (壮鎮)

Meaning: The name consists of the kanji *"sō,"* typically translated as "robust," "vibrancy," "manliness," "manhood," or "strength," and *"chin,"* usually meaning calm and tranquility. Hence two possible translations are "Tranquil Strength," and "Vibrant Calm."

Opening Movement – Opponent Holds Our Garments, with left hand holding our right sleeve (Steps 1 through 5): Pulling our right arm diagonally up and around over his left arm, we release our right arm. Simultaneously, we exert pressure on his right arm by raising our left hand in an *age-uke* like motion. We continue by shifting our free right hand to the outside of his right arm, and release our left arm. To follow up, we hook his right leg with our right arm while extending our left arm over his neck. Pulling his leg up and pressing his neck down, we can throw the opponent to the ground.

The last move – *ge-dan-barai* with one hand and pulling the other hand diagonally upward – is present in several Kata. There are several variations but the principle appears to be the same: throw the opponent to the ground by scooping his leg with one hand (in Kata this hand moves diagonally up) while pressing underneath his chin with the other (in Kata this hand executes *ge-dan-barai*). Indeed, this move represents a minor convention within Kata.

Question: *In which Kata can we find the application of this minor convention?*

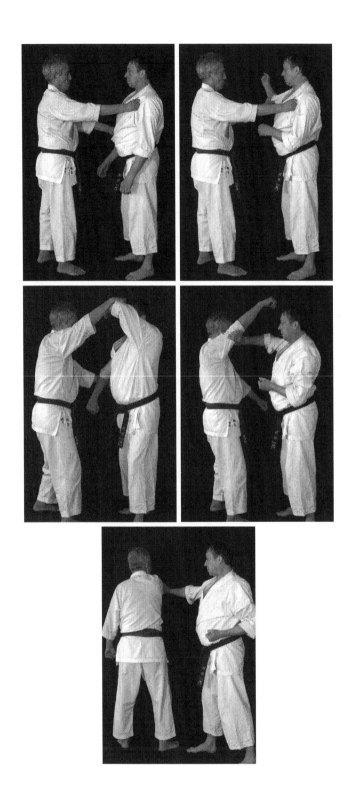

Vignettes from Sō-chin

25 SHŌTŌ-KAN KATA: **STEPS 24-25**
BEST KARATE: **STEPS 24-25**

Opponent Holds Both Our Hands: We grab his right wrist with our right hand and release our left hand by swinging it diagonally up. Then, we release his right hand and catch hold of his left hand with our right. Finally, we raise his right arm upward with our right hand, while pressing his head downward with our left hand to execute a *kaiten-nage* throw.

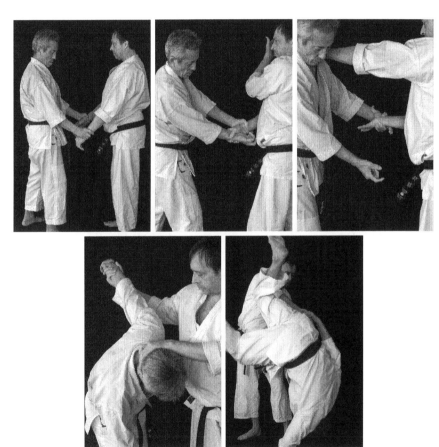

Meikyō (明鏡)

Meaning: Clear Mirror

Opening Movement – Opponent Holds Both Our Hands: Swinging our arms upward with our right hand outside his right hand – we grasp his right hand with our right and pull him down toward our right side. In the process, we will also free our left hand from his grasp. (Naturally, we could perform the entire sequence of movements by swinging our arms outside his left arm and pulling him to our left side.)

Vignettes from Meikyō

25 SHŌTŌ-KAN KATA: **STEPS 26 & 28**

BEST KARATE: **STEPS 26 & 28**

Opponent Holds Our Garments: We perform *tsukuri* to our right with our left arm going over his right and under his left arm. Reversing direction, we swing our left arm upward against his left hand, releasing its hold from our garment. (You may remember we did a similar release from a two-hand hold in the opening move of *Heian Ni-dan*.) At the same time, our right arm swings up in a circular motion towards his neck underneath his chin. (The combined motion of both hands adds power to the release.) Reversing motion, we press his neck with our right arm, throwing him to the ground.

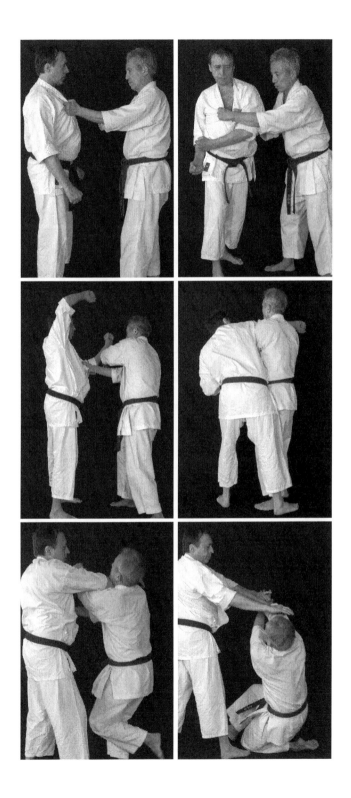

189

Unsu (雲手)

Meaning: Cloud Hands

Opening Movement – Opponent Holds Our Garments (Steps 1 through 2): Performing *tsukuri* to our left, we seize his right arm with both our hands (leverage) from underneath with a forceful upward motion in order to release his grip. If his grip is too strong, we could press against his thumb to facilitate the release. Reversing direction, we push his right hand away while turning him around. A follow-up action

might be to slip our left hand under his jaw while catching him by his right lapel, slip our right arm under his right arm and apply a *kata-ha-jime* choke. We could also apply a rear naked choke (*hadaka-jime*) or any of the nelson-variety choke-holds (*ha-gai-jime*). The foregoing application of *hazushi-waza* can be easily modified to free ourselves from two-hand holds against our hands.

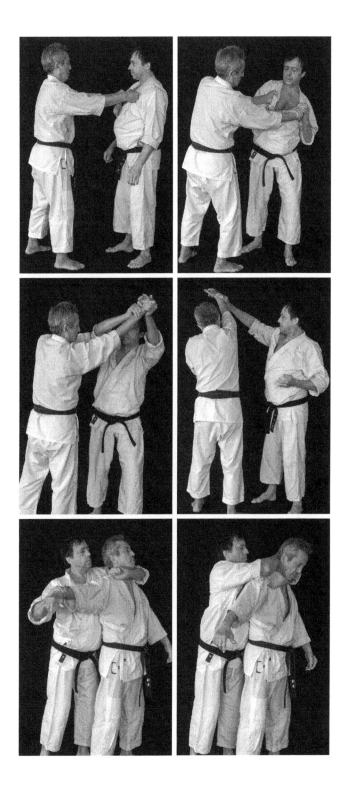

Vignettes from Unsu

25 SHŌTŌ-KAN KATA: **STEPS 2-7**
BEST KARATE: **STEPS 2-7**

Opponent Holds Both Our Hands: Performing *tsukuri* to our left, we slide our right hand underneath his right arm. Reversing direction, we swing our forearm in a circular motion to release our hands. As the opponent is turning so that his back faces us we quickly apply a choking technique from the back.

25 SHŌTŌ-KAN KATA: **STEP 26**
BEST KARATE: **STEPS 30-31**

Opponent Holds Both Our Hands: We place our left hand over his right hand to gain leverage for the release of our right hand, which we raise high above. With our right hand free, we strike his right hand with *"otoshi-zuki,"* releasing our left hand.

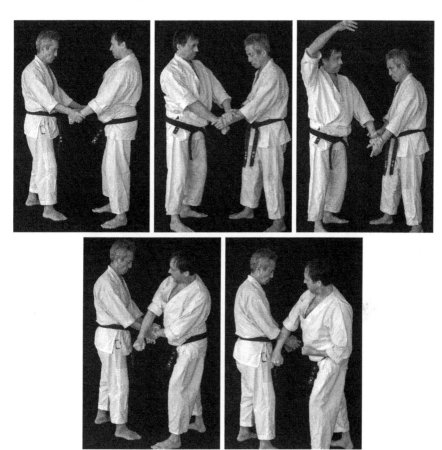

25 SHŌTŌ-KAN KATA:	**STEP 12 & 13**
BEST KARATE:	**STEPS 16 & 17**

Historical Challenge: How has mawashi-geri – *prominently featured in* Unsu – *found its way into the repertoire of* Shōtō-kan *Kata?* Unsu *is an old Kata. Arakaki Seishō (1840-1918), one of Okinawa's early Tō-de heavyweights, was reportedly fond of teaching it. Did the early masters actually practice* mawashi-geri? *Were they even aware of such a technique? Take the* Shitō-ryū *form of the Kata: no roundhouse kick. Apparently, someone unaware of the original purpose of Kata added the kick later, dealing, as a result, a blow to the overall thematic integrity of Kata movements. By way of making amends, let us consider other possible applications of those moves. Would a* kani-basami *throwing technique (scissors throw) be more appropriate? After all, it can be used effectively as* hazushi-waza.

Bassai Shō (抜塞小)

Meaning: Seizing a Fortress – Minor/Small

Former/Other Name: *Passai Shō*

Proposed New Meaning: Slipping out of a Small Fortress

Opening Movement – Opponent Holds Both Our Hands: Performing *tsukuri* to our left, we slip our right hand over his left hand aiming at catching his right hand. At the same time, we slip out from his hold with our left hand which simultaneously catches hold of his left hand. Up to now, this preparation is the same as for *jū-ji-nage*. In this case, however, we turn the opponent around just like in the opening movement of *Heian Yon-dan*, placing him in a vulnerable position.

Vignettes from Bassai Shō

25 SHŌTŌ-KAN KATA:	**STEP 28 & 29**
BEST KARATE:	**STEPS 26 & 27**

Opponent Holds Both Our Hands: We rotate the wrist of our right hand to face his hand from the outside while swinging our arm upward in a circle and pushing on his arm with the palm of our right hand (this course is often referred to as *"hito-yama"* (一山). Then, we immediately slip our left hand from under our right arm catching hold of his left arm (*"futa-yama"* (二山)). Continuing in a circular motion we press on his elbow with our right hand, applying an elbow hold such as *ude-gatame* or *neji-daoshi*, as demonstrated by Master Funakoshi in his *Karate Jutsu*.

Kankū Shō (観空小)

Meaning: Looking at the Sky – Major/Big

Proposed New Meaning: Looking at the Small Sky

Opening Movement – Opponent Holds Both Our Hands: Performing *tsukuri* to our right, we swing our left arm over our right fist, and, as the opponent begins to resist our rightward movement, we reverse direction, pushing with our left arm against his left in a *morote-uke*-like motion, accomplishing release of both our hands. The next is a mirror-image movement, as shown on the photographs below.

Vignettes from Kankū Shō

25 SHŌTŌ-KAN KATA: **STEP 4**
BEST KARATE: **STEPS 4a-4b**

Opponent Holds Our Garments: We slip our right arm over his left arm and underneath his right arm in a *tsukuri* motion to the left (in the Kata this motion looks like a straight punch). Reversing direction, we swing our right arm in an *uchi-uke*-like motion, releasing the opponent's grip.

Wankan (王冠)

Meaning: Royal Crown

Opening Movement – Opponent Holds Our Garments: In a deep *tsukuri* to our right, we shift our left arm over the opponent's right arm and extend it underneath his left arm. Reversing direction, we apply *kaki-wake* by pressing with our left arm against his left, freeing ourselves from his grip. The next is a mirror-image movement, as shown on the photographs below.

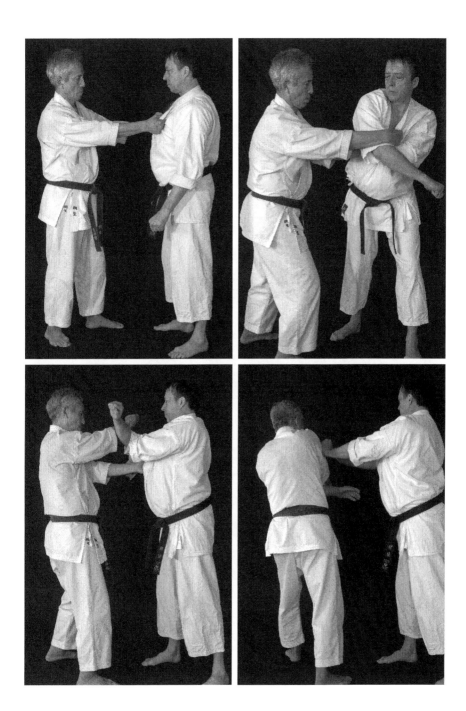

Vignettes from Wankan

25 SHŌTŌ-KAN KATA: STEPS 3-5

Simple Release When an Opponent Holds Both Our Hands: As we raise our forearms – twisting them so that the backs of our fists face forward, more or less as practiced in the Kata – we aim at pushing his left arm with our released left hand (or his right arm with our right hand) away from us into safety. Crossing our forearms as we raise them may be even more effective. (As we lift our arms, we could also strike his right arm with our right (or left arm with our left), releasing our left hand, then releasing our right hand by grabbing and pushing away his left hand with our left hand.)

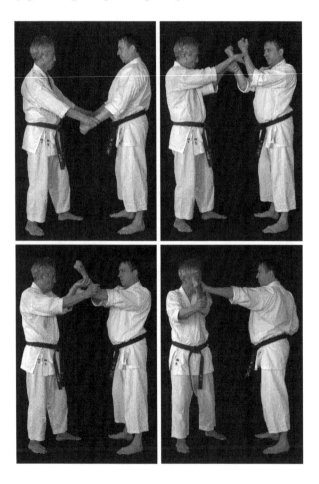

Escape from a Garment Hold: When the opponent catches the lapels of our garments, we get hold of his lapels, pulling him towards us (*tsukuri*). As he resists, we reverse direction, this time pushing him upwards to his left or right (forcing him to shift his weight onto that leg) and execute an ō-*soto-gari* (大外刈) throwing technique against his *sasae-ashi*.

Go-jū-shi-ho Shō (五十四歩小)

Meaning: Fifty-Four Steps – Minor/Small

Opening Movement – Opponent Holds Our Garments: Performing *tsukuri* to our left, we extend our right arm underneath his right and our left arm over his right. Reversing direction, we push his right arm with our right arm, releasing its hold of our garment, and continue pressing his right arm down, turning him away from us. We immediately wrap our left arm around his neck connecting with our right arm (which we could then press against the back of his head) and apply a *hadaka-jime* choking technique. The choking application is the same as in steps 34-37 of *Jion*.

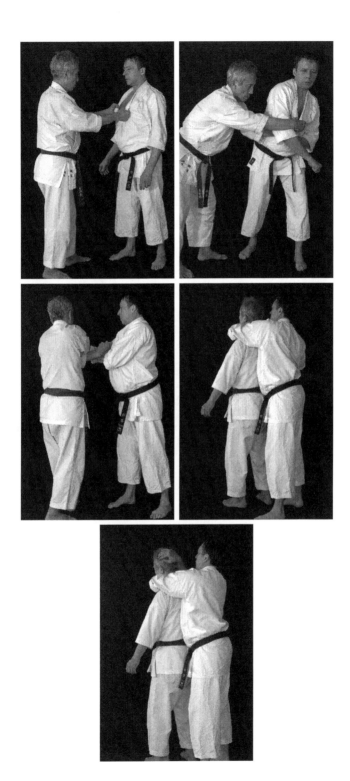

Vignettes from Go-jū-shi-ho Shō

25 SHŌTŌ-KAN KATA: **STEPS 15-16**
BEST KARATE: **STEPS 15-16**

Opponent Holds Both Our Hands: We perform *tsukuri* to our left while catching hold of the opposite hands of the opponent in preparation for a *jū-ji-nage.*

Go-jū-shi-ho Dai (五十四歩大)

Meaning: Fifty-Four Steps – Major/Big

Opening Movement – Opponent Holds Our Garments: Same as for *Go-jū-shi-ho Shō*, as described above.

Vignettes from Go-jū-shi-ho Dai

25 SHŌTŌ-KAN KATA: **STEPS 2-3**
BEST KARATE: **STEPS 2-3**

Opponent Holds Both Our Hands: We perform *tsukuri* to our right, swinging our left arm over his right arm and releasing his grip. We continue the circular motion of our arms, pushing his hands upward from underneath, releasing his grip on our right hand, and pushing his arms up and to the side.

Raising our straight arms alone toward his shoulders (pushing his shoulders up) could also be an effective technique against a two-hand hold.

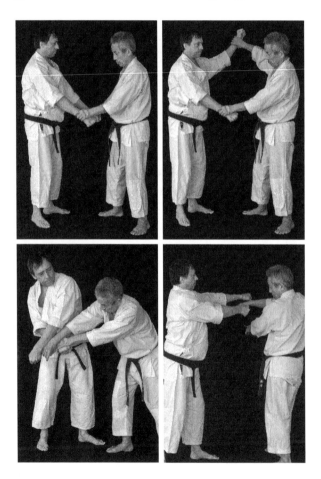

Glossary

Age-uke (揚受), a rising block.

Age-zuki (揚突), a rising punch.

Aiki-otoshi (合気落とし), an *"aiki"* drop-throwing technique.

Ashi (足), a foot or a leg.

Awase-zuki (合突), a "U"-shaped double punch.

Budō (武道), the Way of the Warrior.

Bugei (武芸), martial arts; as in *"Karate ha kunshi no bugei"* (空手は君子の武芸), translated as "Karate is the martial arts of a true gentleman," one of favorite sayings of Master Funakoshi.

Bunbu Ryōdō (文武両道), pursuit of a dual path, embracing both literary and martial arts.

Bunkai (分解), analyzing and finding applications of Kata techniques.

Chakra, one of several major outlets/entry points of *Ki* into our bodies, especially one of seven such points located along our spinal column.

Choku-zuki (直突), a straight punch.

Chū-dan (中段), middle section (of the body).

Dan (段), a rank in Karate above *kyu* level, traditionally ranging from *sho-dan* (初段) to *jū-dan* (十段).

De-ai (出会い), attacking upon commitment or initiation of action (*okori*) by the partner.

De-ashi-barai (出足払い), a foot-sweeping throwing technique.

Dō-gi (道着), a Karate uniform, universally referred to in English as *"gi."*

Dōjō (道場), a place where Karate (and other *Budō* arts) are regularly practiced.

Ein (会陰), an acupuncture point located on the Conception Vessel meridian typically designated as CV1 and referred to in English as the *Meeting of Yin* place; at *ein* three powerful acupuncture channels emerge from the body: the Conception Vessel, the Governing Vessel and the Penetrating Vessel.

Embusen (演武線), a directional pattern for the performance of Kata.

Enpi (-uchi) (猿臂(打)), an elbow (strike); (same meaning as *hiji-ate*).

Fudō-dachi (不動立), an immovable (rooted) stance, also referred to as *sō-chin-dachi*.

Fumi-ashi (踏み足), stepping action characterized by bringing thighs together during movement rather than moving legs in a straight line.

Fumi-komi (踏み込み), stomping the floor to increase the power and speed of a technique.

Furi-zuki (振突), a swinging punch.

Ge-dan-barai (下段払), a downward sweeping block.

Gedatsu (解脱), a state of being free of earthly desires; a state of nothingness.

Gedatsu-hō (解脱法), means of escape from grappling holds.

Go-no-sen (後の先), taking action (such as an attack, a blocking attack, or a block with a following attack) after the partner has initiated execution of a technique.

Gyaku-jū-ji-jime (逆十字絞), a "reverse cross strangle" – a choking technique done by grasping the partner's lapels from the inside with our hands placed in a crossed position (with palms facing outwards) and pressing on his carotid arteries.

Gyaku-zuchi (逆槌), a "reverse hammer" throw; one of the throwing techniques included in Master Funakoshi's textbooks; the kanji have alternate pronunciations, including *"saka-zuchi."*

Gyaku-zuki (逆突), a reverse punch.

Hachi-ji-dachi (八字立), a natural open-leg stance in which the position of the feet resembles the shape of the Chinese character *hachi* (八).

Hadaka-jime (裸絞), a rear naked choke.

Ha-gai-jime (羽交い絞), any of the nelson-type grappling holds/ choking techniques.

Haitō (背刀), a ridge hand.

Haiwan-nagashi-uke (背腕流し受), a back-arm sweeping block.

Haiwan-uke (背腕受), a back-arm block.

Hangetsu-dachi (半月立), half-moon stance.

Hanka-fuza (半跏趺坐), a half-lotus position for sitting *zazen*.

Hanmi (半身), a body position with hips turned sideways.

Hazushi-waza (外し技), techniques for escaping from holds and grabs.

Heikō-dachi (平行立), a parallel stance.

Heisoku-dachi (閉足立), a stance with feet side by side and touching.

Hen-shu (変手), switching the *ki-sei* conditions of hands, as in switching the *shini-te* state of a forward hand to the *iki-te* state in preparation for an attack.

Hiji-ate (肘当), an elbow strike (same meaning as *enpi-uchi*).

Hiji-uke (肘受), an elbow block; an application of this block can be found in *Heian San-dan* and *Gankaku* Kata.

Hiki-te (引き手), the pulling hand helping turbocharge the release of *Ki* through the hand performing a technique while maintaining a Yin-and-Yang balance within the autonomous unit consisting of both hands; *hiki-te* can also be used to grab the opponent in order to imbalance them or add additional power to our strikes while simultaneously pulling the opponent toward us.

Hira-kake-te (平掛け手), a block using the thumb side of the wrist, ending with palm facing up; an application of this block can be found in *Hangetsu*.

Hira-ken (平拳), a four-knuckle fist, literally a "flat fist;" it is formed by bending only the 2nd and 3rd knuckles of four fingers, while keeping the hand otherwise flat.

Hiraki-uke (開き受け), a double outward block with thumb sides of forearms (the name *hiraki* deriving from *hiraku* (開く), meaning to open), an application of this block can be found in a number of Kata, including *Gankaku, Meikyo, Chin-te* and *Jion*.

Hira-nuki-te (ひら貫手), a spear-hand with palm facing up.

212

Hokkai-jō-in (法界定印), a meditation mudra of the Dharma Realm traditionally used during *zazen*.

Hyaku-e (百会), an acupuncture point located on top of the head; translated into English as "hundred convergences."

Ibuki (息吹), literally "breath;" patterns of inhaling and exhaling during Karate training or when executing Karate techniques. The term is often used in reference to exhaling. Practice of *ibuki* is often accompanied by emission of various sounds (*kiai*).

Iki-te (活き手), a Yang-*Ki* energized hand ready for action – typically a hand pulled back slightly, in contrast to *shini-te*, a hand normally used for blocking – typically a leading hand; a "live" hand.

Inen (意念), a thought, feeling, consciousness, or intention; focusing *inen* on an object or part of a body will activate *Ki* there.

Ippon-ken (一本拳), a fist with the second knuckle of the index finger protruding; a one-knuckle fist.

Ippon-nuki-te (一本貫手), a hand with the index finger protruding straight while the other fingers are bent at the second knuckles.

Irimi-nage (入り身投げ), an "entering" throw – one of the rudimentary throws of Aikido.

Jiku-ashi (軸足), a pivot leg.

Jiyū kumite (自由組手), free sparring, typically governed by many rules to assure fairness to and protect the safety of the participants.

Jō-dan (上段), upper section (face).

Jō-tanden (上丹田), upper *tanden* located inside our foreheads between the eyebrows slightly above the bridge of our nose.

Jū-ji-nage (十字投げ), a throw executed by crossing the partner's arms at the elbows.

Jū-ji-uke (十字受), a crossed-wrists block.

Jun-zuki (順突), a lunge punch; an alternative term for *oi-zuki*.

Jutsu (術), a technique.

Kagi-zuki (鉤突), a hook punch.

Kake-uke (掛け受け), a middle hooking block, rarely practiced in the *Shōtō-kan* system; similar techniques, referred to as *maki-otoshi-uke* and *sukui-uke*, appear in *Ni-jū-shi-ho* and *Unsu*.

Kaiten-nage (回転投げ), a "rotary" throw made by pushing the partner's head downward while rotating their arm up behind their back.

Kaki-wake (-uke) (搔分(受)), a technique for breaking the opponent's hold with the ulnar sides of the forearms by pushing their arm(s) away; a derivative of the word *kakiwakeru*, meaning to push away/aside, to elbow one's way through.

Kakutō (鶴頭), a bent wrist.

Kamae (構え), usually refers to ready stances of Karate practitioners engaged in *kumite*; the term also refers to the opening stances of Kata.

Kani-basami (蟹挟), a scissors throw.

Kansetsu-waza (関節技), joint-locking techniques.

Karami (or *–garami*, in compound words) (絡み), an entanglement, a term applied to various *kansetsu-waza*.

Karate-dō (空手道), the way of Karate; the concept of fully embracing and pursuing Karate as a way of life in all its manifestations, including its moral, mental, social and spiritual aspects.

Karate-ka (空手家), a practitioner of Karate.

Kata (型) or (形), a thematic composition of Karate techniques applying soft and hard, slow and fast application of power; each Kata begins and ends with a bow (*rei*).

Kata (肩), a shoulder.

Kata-ashi-dori (片足取り), a single-leg-grab throwing technique.

Kata-guruma (肩車), a shoulder-wheel throwing technique.

Kata-ha-jime (片羽絞), a "single-wing" choking technique.

Katame (or –*gatame*, in compound words) (固め), a term signifying a hold, lock or tightening in holding/grappling techniques.

Katame-waza (固め技), grappling or holding techniques.

Kata-wa-guruma (片輪車), literally a misshaped, deformed or disfigured wheel; a throwing technique that looks like an incomplete *kata-guruma*.

Keiko (稽古), a training, practice or study of Karate (as well as other arts).

Keiraku (経絡), meridian(s), major Ki pathways throughout our bodies.

Keitō (鶏頭), a chicken-head wrist.

Kekka-fuza (結跏趺坐), a full-lotus position for sitting *zazen*.

Ken (拳), a fist; standing alone this Chinese character is normally pronounced *kobushi* in Japanese.

Ken (剣), a sword.

Ken-sei (拳聖), a "saint of the fist," a "fist saint."

Ken-sei (剣聖), a "saint of the sword."

Ken-tsui (拳槌), a hammer-fist (ulnar side of fist); same as *tettsui*.

Keri (蹴り), a kick.

Keri-waza (蹴り技), kicking techniques.

Ki (気), the conscious energy from which each of us and everything else in the cosmos is being created.

Kiai (気合), a sound emitted while performing forced *ibuki*.

Kiba-dachi (騎馬立), a horse-riding stance, also referred to as a straddle-leg stance.

Kihon (基本), the basics; *kihon* practice consists of repetitive practice of basic Karate techniques and their combinations, including punches, blocks and kicks. Traditionally, Karate practice consists of *kihon*, Kata and *kumite*.

Kikō (気功), breathing exercises; the term is also translated as Qigong.

Kime (決め), an explosive, laser-like focus of *Ki* through the target of a technique upon impact, characterized by a strong contraction of the lower back and *tanden* and an explosive *ibuki*.

Kinhin (経行), *zazen* meditation performed while walking.

Ki-sei (奇正), a reference to both hands, one of which (typically the front hand) is a "*ki*" or "strange" hand devoid of Yang energy (hence also called *shini-te* or "dead" hand) (for example, a hand that just completed a punch);

the other is a *"sei"* or *"proper"* hand, ie hand that is Yang-*Ki*-energized and ready for action (hence also called *iki-te* or "live" hand).

Kizami-zuki (刻み突), a jab with the leading hand.

Kōhai (後輩), a person who is junior to another in a particular social situation.

Kō-kutsu-dachi (後屈立), a back stance.

Kokyū-nage (呼吸投げ), a "breath" throw, one of the rudimentary throwing techniques of Aikido.

Kubi-wa (首環), an encircling-the-neck throw, also known as *kubi-nage*.

Kuden (口伝), oral tradition.

Kuma-de (熊手), a "bear hand," formed by bending fingers at their second knuckles.

Kumite (組手), a Karate sparring, either prearranged or impromptu.

Kun-yomi (訓読み), Japanese readings of kanji.

Kyū (級), a beginning Karate rank below *dan* level culminating with first *kyū*, or *ikkyū* (一級).

Kyū-sho (急所), vital points along our bodies.

Mae-enpi (-uchi) (前猿臂(打)), a forward horizontal elbow (strike).

Mae-geri (前蹴), a front kick.

Ma-ai (間合), distance or space between partners or opponents facing each other.

Maki-otoshi-uke (巻き落とし受け), downward swirling block with the ulnar side of the wrist hooking from above.

Maki-wara (巻藁), an implement or structure, such as a wooden post, designed for striking, kicking or executing other Karate techniques; the striking part can be made of plaited straw but more commonly is made of leather or padded cloth.

Mawashi-geri (回蹴), a roundhouse kick.

Mawashi-zuki (回突), a roundhouse punch.

Me-sen (目線), an eye vector.

Mete (雌手), a "female hand," also referred to as *shini-te*.

Mikiri (見切り), moving just beyond the opponent' range of incoming attack.

Morote-gari (双手刈), a throw made by grabbing both of the opponents legs with two hands from the front; *see ude-wa*.

Morote-uke (諸手受), an augmented forearm block.

Mu (無), "nothingness" (also "not to have" or "be without"); a key concept in Buddhism and in particular its *zen* traditions.

Musubi-dachi (結び立), a stance with heels touching and feet turned outward at approximately 45 degrees.

Nagashi-uke (流し受), a guiding block.

Nage-waza (投げ技), throwing techniques.

Naka-daka-ippon-ken (中高一本拳), a fist with the second knuckle of the middle finger protruding.

Nami-jū-ji-jime (並十字絞), a "normal cross strangle" – a choking technique done by grasping the partner's lapels from the outside, with our hands placed in a crossed position (with palms inwards) and pressing on their carotid arteries.

Neko-ashi-dachi (猫足立), a cat stance.

Nige (逃げ), escaping out of the opponent's *uchima* in reaction to their movement.

Nuki-te (貫手), a spear hand.

Oi-komi (追い込み), techniques for "pursuing" the opponent.

Oi-zuki (追突), a punch while stepping forward with the same hand as your leading leg.

Okori (起こり), initiation, beginning (of a movement).

On-yomi (音読み), Chinese readings of kanji.

Osae-uke (押え受), a pressing block.

Ō-soto-gari (大外刈), a throwing technique made by sweeping the opponent's leg from outside in a reaping back-to-front motion (by using right leg against his right leg or left leg against his left leg).

Ote (雄手), a "male hand," also referred to as *iki-te*.

Rei (礼), a bow, showing respect for a place or person; we bow when entering and exiting a *dōjō*, and we bow to our partners during Karate exercises.

Re-no-ji-dachi (レの字立), an "L" stance, in which the position of the feet resembles the shape of the katakana character "レ".

Renshū (練習), training, practice.

Rō-kyū (労宮), a *tsubo* point located in the middle of our palms (PC 8 on the meridian/acupoint chart).

Sae (冴え), sharpness or clarity; the term can be applied in reference to sharpness of a technique or in the context of refining its *kime*.

San-chin-dachi (三戦立), an hour-glass stance.

Sasae-ashi (支え足), a supporting leg.

Seika-tanden (臍下丹田), usually referred to simply as *tanden* (丹田) or lower *tanden* (*ge-tanden* (下丹田)), is the pit of the stomach and center of our gravity which we concentrate on during Karate exercises (and ideally at all times); among various other names, it is also referred to as *sei-tanden* (正丹田), or proper/correct *tanden*.

Seiken (正拳), a basic fist formation with four fingers tightly clenched (or three fingers clenched with index finger from second knuckle extended) and overlapped with the thumb; literally a "proper fist."

Sei-ryū-tō (青竜刀), literally a "blue dragon sword," an ox-jaw hand.

Seiza (正座), literally, "proper/correct sitting," a traditional Japanese sitting manner with legs folded underneath the thighs and big toes overlapping; traditionally women sit with knees together, but men sit with knees separated; this is the proper sitting position in a Karate *dōjō* and can be used for sitting *zazen*.

Sen-no-sen (先の先), taking preemptive action (such as a block or an attack) upon manifestation of intention to attack and before such intention takes on a physical execution by the partner.

Senpai (先輩), a person who is senior to another in a particular social situation; a person can be senior in one respect (eg age) but junior in another (eg Karate rank).

Sensei (先生), a teacher.

Shiai (試合), a match, contest, competition.

Shidō-in (指導員), an instructor.

Shihan (師範), a grand master, teacher, master, instructor.

Shiko-dachi (四股立), a square stance.

Shime-waza (絞め技), choking techniques.

Shin (心), mind, heart, spirit; *on-yomi* of *kokoro*.

Shini-te (死に手), a Yin-*Ki* energized hand – typically the leading hand normally used for blocking, in contrast to *iki-te*, a hand ready for action.

Shōmen (正面), a body position with hips facing squarely to the front.

Shu-tō (手刀), a knife-hand.

Shu-tō-uchi (手刀打), a knife-hand strike.

Shu-tō-uke (手刀受), a knife-hand block.

Sō-chin-dachi (壮鎮立ち), a diagonal straddle-leg stance, also referred to as *fudō-dachi*.

Soto-uke (外受け), an outside block (from outside inward); as I understand it, outside of *Shōtō-kan*, this block is referred to as *uchi-uke*.

Sukui-nage (掬投), a leg-scooping throwing technique (*sukū*, 掬う, meaning to scoop).

Sukui-uke (掬受け), a scooping block.

Sun-dome (寸止め), the principle of stopping an attack short of reaching the target, signifying the no-contact aspect of Karate practice; *"sun"* refers to a traditional length unit in Japan equal to about 30 millimeters or 1.2 inches, and *"dome"* comes from the verb *tomeru*, to stop.

Suri-ashi (摺り足), shifting or adjusting position relative to the partner by sliding feet along the floor/ground without taking a step; the *"suri"* character of *suri-ashi* derives from *suru*, meaning to rub; also called *yori-ashi*.

Tai (体), body, substance; *on-yomi* of *karada*.

Tai-otoshi (体落), a body-drop throwing technique with the help of a leg extended in front of the partner's leg.

Tai-sabaki (体捌き), shifting the body out of the line of attack.

Tanden (丹田), see *seika-tanden* above.

Tate-enpi (-uchi) (縦猿臂(打)), a vertical elbow (strike) (*tate* meaning "vertical).

Tate-ken (縦拳), a vertical fist.

Tate-(ken)-zuki (縦(拳)突), a punch with a vertical fist.

Te (手), (1) a hand or hands (in compound words often pronounced as *shu* or *de*); (2) a term describing martial arts systems in Okinawa; as many aspects of *Te* were introduced from China, Okinawans referred to what was later to be known as Karate as *Tō-de* (唐手), meaning literally "Tang hands" or "Chinese hands;" variants of *Te* would be identified by references to the places where they were commonly practiced, such as *Shuri-te*, *Tomari-te*, or *Naha-te*.

Tegumi (手組), a form of wrestling popular among children in Okinawa during Master Funakoshi's younger days.

Tei-shō (底掌), a palm heel.

Tei-shō-uchi (底掌打ち), a palm-heel strike.

Tettsui (鉄槌), a hammer-fist (ulnar side of fist) (*tettsui* meaning "iron hammer"); same as *ken-tsui*.

Tsubo (壺), effective acupuncture (or moxa) points along the meridian lines of our bodies.

Tsugi-ashi (継足), taking a step with the leading foot by first shifting the back foot forward usually to close the distance toward the opponent; *Hangetsu* Kata provides an illustration of *tsugi-ashi* application.

Tsuki (突き), a punch or thrust.

Tsuki-uke (突き受け), a punching block (or a blocking punch).

Tsuki-waza (突き技), punching or thrusting techniques.

Tsukuri (作り), in methods of escape, a preparatory maneuver causing our partner to counter-react in the direction of our intended action; "setting up" or positioning the partner so that their reaction facilitates performance of our intended action; applied along the line of Funakoshi-sensei's advice on methods of escape that in order to go West, we first go East.

Uchi (打ち), a strike.

Uchi-ma (打間), a striking range; a distance within which our technique can reach the opponent.

Uchi-uke (内受け), an inner block (from inside outward); as I understand it, outside of *Shōtō-kan*, this block is referred to as *soto-uke*.

Uchi-waza (打ち技), striking techniques.

Ude (腕), an arm.

Ude-garami (腕絡) (腕縅), a bent arm lock.

Ude-gatame (腕固), an arm grappling hold.

Ude-kujiki (腕挫き), twisting and pressing an arm downward (*kujiku* means to sprain, wrench or dislocate).

Ude-wa (腕環), literally an "arm circle/ring;" a double-leg takedown not unlike *morote-gari* (双手刈) of Judo; one of the several throws demonstrated by Master Funakoshi in his written works.

Uke (受け), a technique, often translated as a block, for receiving, neutralizing, redirecting or deflecting *Ki* of the opponent's attack; it can be applied as a guiding, redirecting, pressing, smashing, scooping, hooking, attacking, or movement-arresting block.

Ukemi (受身), break-falling techniques.

Ura-ken (裏拳), a back-fist.

Ura-ken-uchi (裏拳打), a back-fist strike.

Ura-zuki (裏突), a punch with the palm side of the fist up; a close punch.

Washi-de (鷲手)、an eagle-hand formed by pressing fingertips and a thumb together, resembling the shape of a bird's beak.

Waza (技), a technique; pronounced *"gi"* in *on-yomi*.

Yakusoku kumite (約束組手), prearranged sparring.

Yama-zuki (山突), or *Irimi-awase-zuki* (入り身合突), a vertical double punch, sometimes referred to as a U-punch.

Yoko-geri-keage (横蹴/蹴上), a side snap kick.

Yori-ashi (寄り足), same as *suri-ashi*; the *"yori"* character of *yori-ashi* derives from *yoru*, meaning to approach or draw near, implying advancing; in current usage, however, both terms – *suri-ashi* and *yori-ashi* – tend to function interchangeably.

Yūdansha (有段者), a person(s) holding a black belt in martial arts.

Yū-sen (湧泉), a *tsubo* point located in the depression of the heart of the foot's sole commonly referred to as bubbling or gushing springs (KI 1 on the meridian/acupoint chart).

Zafu (座蒲), a cushion for sitting *zazen*.

Zanshin (残心), a continuous and conscious projection of *Ki* following the execution of a technique; *zanshin* continues until the technique is fully (not just physically) complete.

Zen-kutsu-dachi (前屈立), a front (forward) stance (with front leg bent).

Zuki (突き), an alternative reading of *"tsuki"* (a punch) in many compound words where another character or characters appear in front of it.

About the Author

Adam Newhouse, a long-term resident of Japan, got his first taste of martial arts on Judo mats during primary school. After Judo, he took up Karate and has practiced in Shotokan dojos for four decades. Karate is a lifelong journey for Adam. He never stops questioning, studying and exploring to deepen his knowledge of the art and to gain insight into its hidden applications. An episode in his Karate life in Japan gives a glimpse of Adam's passion and dedication. A favorite teacher, Osaka Yoshiharu-sensei, was teaching the *Hyaku-Hachi* (108) Kata – a rarity in any Shotokan dojo. But that brief introduction only whetted Adam's appetite. Inspired to learn the Kata thoroughly, he secretly studied the *Suparinpei* (108) Kata at a Goju-ryu dojo for more than seven years. Adam can be reached at Adam@black-belts-only.com

Made in the USA
Middletown, DE
26 November 2017